Amigurumi Crochet Patterns for Beginners

33 Cute & Easy Crochet Amigurumi Animals Patterns For Beginners With Step By Step Instructions & Illustrations

Nancy Gordon

Contents

Introduction v

    Basic Instructions 9
    What You Need for Amigurumi................................. 20
    Abbreviations Used in the Book: 22

Chapter 1: The Sea Animals 23

    Dreamy the Starfish 23
    Twirl the Octopus..27
    Gillian the Jellyfish 30
    Wally the Whale 33
    Billy the Turtle 36
    Cheri the Crab 39
    Kate the Clown Fish 42

Chapter 2: The Home Buddies 46

    Cleo the Chic 46
    Mike the Mouse...49
    Tuffy the Dog 51
    Snips the Bunny 56
    Tina the Pusheen Cat 60

Chapter 3: The Farm Animals................................. 64

    Sheila the Sheep..64
    Paulie the Pig 67
    Pru the Alpaca 70
    Dina the Duck 74

Chapter 4: The Wild Ones.. 78

    Holly the Hippo 78
    Rob the Rhino 81
    Abi the Elephant 85
    Vicky the Bear 90
    Jolly the Reindeer 94

Carl the Tiger 99
Huan the Panda 104
Walty the Lion 109
Charlie the Baby Dinosaur 114

Chapter 5: The Cuties 118

Grace the Caterpillar 118
Oscar the Owl 122
Ginnie the Ladybug 125
Trisha the Bee 128
Bernie the Bat 131

Chapter 6: Big Size Animals 134

Mr. Big Bunny 134
Mr. Gary the Giraffe 140
Mr. Rob the Rooster 146

Conclusion 159

The Therapeutic Benefits of Crocheting 159

References 162

© **Copyright 2021 by Nancy Gordon - All rights reserved.**

The content contained within this book may not be reproduced, duplicated or transmitted without direct written permission from the author or the publisher.

Under no circumstances will any blame or legal responsibility be held against the publisher, or author, for any damages, reparation, or monetary loss due to the information contained within this book, either directly or indirectly.

Legal Notice:

This book is copyright protected. It is only for personal use. You cannot amend, distribute, sell, use, quote or paraphrase any part, or the content within this book, without the consent of the author or publisher.

Disclaimer Notice:

Please note the information contained within this document is for educational and entertainment purposes only. All effort has been executed to present accurate, up to date, reliable, complete information. No warranties of any kind are declared or implied. Readers acknowledge that the author is not engaged in the rendering of legal, financial, medical or professional advice. The content within this book has been derived from various sources. Please consult a licensed professional before attempting any techniques outlined in this book.

By reading this document, the reader agrees that under no circumstances is the author responsible for any losses, direct or indirect, that are incurred as a result of the use of the information contained within this document, including, but not limited to, errors, omissions, or inaccuracies.

Introduction

Amigurumi is a Japanese art form. Literally, the term means "a crocheted/knitted stuffed toy." The use of yarn and needles to create intricate and cute toys has been a decades old tradition in Japan. It has now received global recognition with crocheters interested in creating unique stuffed toys.

Using yarn or thread and basic crochet stitches, it is easy to work up stuffed animals, dolls, fantasy creatures, etc. Depending on the yarn used, the finished product can be large or small. The crochet hooks normally used for amigurumi include sizes up to 3.5mm. This gives the finished product a smooth look without any of the stuffing showing through gaping holes. Other necessary supplies include embroidery needles to sew up the finished item, polyfill to stuff the toy, and safety eyes/googly eyes as accessories.

The finished crocheted toys are cute to look at and perfect for kids. With button eyes, rosy cheeks and a wonderful smile, every amigurumi toy can bring immense pleasure. Creating them for the holidays or for birthdays is a nice way to gift something special for your kids or grandkids. These are treasure pieces that will become heirlooms.

So, start with the basics of amigurumi and weave some magic into your creations. Start a tradition with your kids and grandkids and see how the love manifested as handmade gifts surpasses all the anonymity of store bought toys.

Crochet Amigurumi is a treasure trove of 33 animal patterns, carefully selected for you. This book is perfect for those who love to crochet and DIY. The patterns included are simple enough for beginners, as well. With colorful designs and clear instructions, we are sure you will find them exciting to create. The cute animal designs illustrated in the book are delightful. Create all 30 and you will have a collection of cuddly animals all ready to have fun with. Discover the joy of amigurumi with this colorful illustrated book!

If you are a beginner crocheter, don't fret! This book has been made for amigurumi newbies as well as crocheters at all experience levels. So, if you would like to start off with some simple patterns, this book is just for you.

The book begins with the basics of crochet stitches to help you get started. The abbreviations used in the book are explained on the Basic Instructions page. This will make it easy for you to read the individual patterns. Once you know the basic crochet stitches, it is easy to move on to the techniques of amigurumi. You just need to wrap your head around working in circles and creating pieces that will join together to form toys.

The book also gives seasoned crocheters a chance to work with some great patterns. So you can make use of your knowledge of crochet and then accessorize the toys to make them your own. Every pattern written here has been checked twice and so you should be able to create the toys with ease.

We have divided the book into sections, with each section beginning with easy patterns. Choose from animals of the sea, home buddies, farm friends, wild ones, and the cuties. Each section has at least four animals to choose from.

With a name for each animal, we love to make the experience a personal one. You can, however, choose to name your toys yourself.

There are seven sea creatures that you can work on. From a dazzling starfish to a silly clownfish, you can choose any one that attracts your attention. Then, we move to the home buddies that are our lovely pets. Again, the patterns are simple to begin with. So Cleo the Chick and Mike the Mouse are quick to crochet. Step into the farm and you will find four animals to crochet. Sheila the Sheep and Paulie the Pig are waiting for you.

Once you are comfortable crocheting these animals, you can move on to the wild animals. We have a whole range of wild ones for you to choose from. Try out the hippo, elephant, bear, lion and tiger, as well as a baby dinosaur. You see, we haven't left many behind! Your kids will be thrilled with the wide range of animals that you can create easily.

The fifth of the book is dedicated to those little cuties that fill our hearts with love. Colorful and vibrant bugs and bees, as well as an owl and a bat, complete the set.

As for the last chapter, it's all about Mr. Big Bunny and Mr. Gary the Giraffe. These are large animals. Finally, don't forget to also check the therapeutic benefits of crocheting in the conclusion.

So, get started with this lovely book and become a pro at amigurumi!

Basic Instructions

How to Do a Slip Knot:

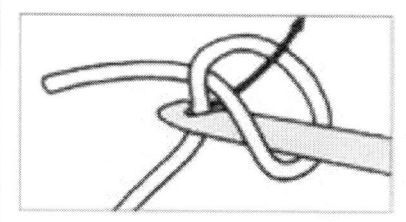 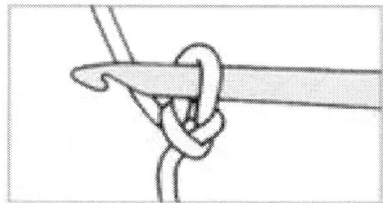

Start by creating a loop with the yarn. Insert the crochet hook through the center of the loop and hook the free end. Pull this through and up onto the working area of the crochet hook. Pull the free yarn end to tighten the loop. The loop on the crochet hook should be firm. Now you have created a slip knot.

How to Do a Slip Stitch (sl st):

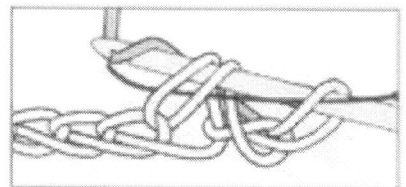 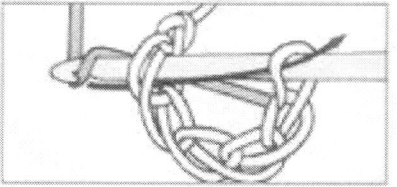

Slip stitch is used to join work in rounds or to move across a row without adding any height.

To do a row of slip stitches, turn your work and chain 1. This is not a turning chain and so you will work on the first stitch as well. Insert the crochet hook in the first stitch and pull the yarn over. Draw the yarn through both the loops of the stitch and on the hook. One slip stitch has been completed. Continue to slip stitch in each of the remaining stitches.

How to Do a Chain Stitch (ch):

 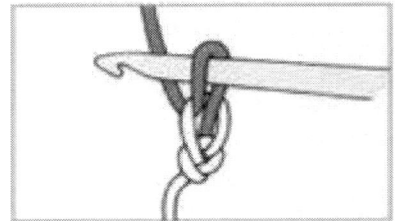

After creating the slip knot, bring the yarn over the crochet hook from back to front and hook it. Draw the hooked yarn through the loop of the slip knot on the hook and up the working area of the crochet hook. One chain stitch created.

Again, hold the base of the slip knot and bring the yarn over the crochet hook from back to front. Hook it and draw through the loop on the hook. Another chain stitch created. Repeat this step to create additional chains.

How to Do a Single Crochet (sc):

 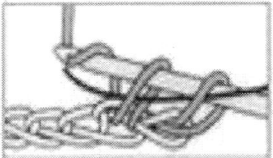 

Make a chain of six. Skip the first chain from the crochet hook, insert the hook in the second chain through the center and under the back bar. Bring the yarn over the hook from the back to the front. Draw yarn through the chain and up onto the working area of the crochet hook. You have two loops on the hook. Bring the yarn over the hook from the back to front, and draw it through both loops on the crochet hook. One loop remains on the hook. One single crochet has been created.

Insert the hook into the next chain. Hook the yarn from back to front and draw it through the chain stitch. Take the yarn over again and draw through both loops. Repeat this step in each of the next chains. One completed row of single crochet is created.

To work the next row of single crochet, turn your work so that you are working on the back. Do a chain 1, which is called the turning chain. Now insert the hook in the last stitch of the previous row under the top two loops. Bring the yarn over the hook from back to front and draw yarn through the stitch and up the working area of the crochet hook. You have two loops on the hook. Bring the yarn over the hook and draw it through both loops on the crochet hook. Work a single crochet in each sc to the end.

How to Do a Half Double Crochet (hdc):

Figure 1

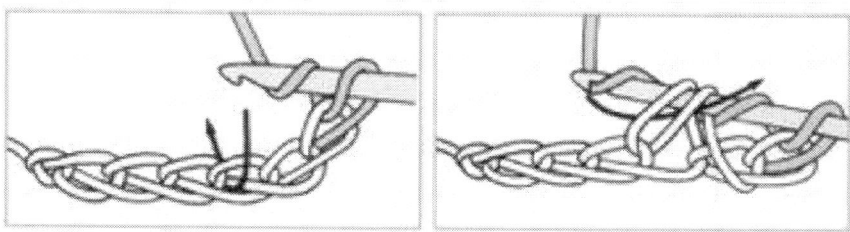

Figure 2

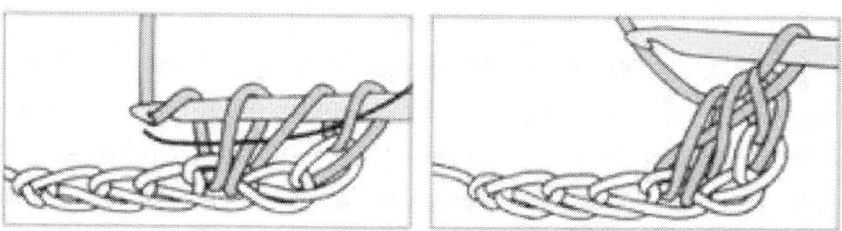

Make a chain of 15. Bring the yarn over the crochet hook from back to front. Skip the first two chains and then insert the hook in the third chain from the hook. Bring the yarn over the crochet hook and draw it through the chain stitch and up onto the working area of the hook. You have now three loops on the hook. Bring the yarn over the crochet hook and draw it through all three loops on the hook. You have completed one half double crochet. Continue to work a half double crochet in each remaining chain.

To work the next row of half double crochet, turn your work so that you are working on the back. Do a chain 2, which is called your turning chain. This turning chain is now your first half double crochet of the next row. So start working in the second stitch onwards. Continue to do a half double crochet in each remaining stitch across. Count your stitches so that you have the right number of half double crochets in each row.

How to Do a Double Crochet (dc):

Figure 1

Figure 2

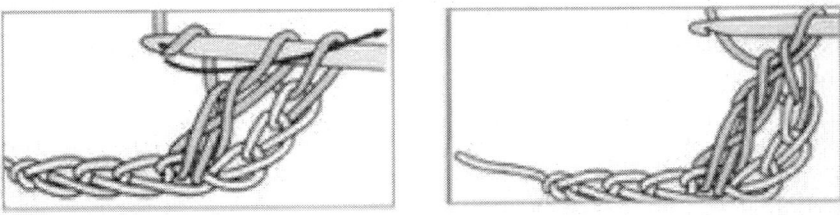

Make a chain of 15. Bring the yarn over the hook from back to front, skip the first three chains from the hook and then insert the hook in the fourth chain. Bring the yarn over the crochet hook from back to front and draw it through the chain stitch and up to the working area of the hook. You have three loops on the hook. Bring the yarn over the crochet hook from back to front and draw through the first two loops on the hook. You now have two loops on the hook. Bring the yarn over the crochet hook from back to front and draw through both loops on the hook. One completed double crochet. Continue to double crochet in each of the remaining chains.

To work the next row of double crochet, turn your work so that you are working on the back. Do a chain 3, which is called your turning chain. This turning chain is now your first double crochet of the next row. So start working in the second stitch onwards. Continue to do a double crochet in each remaining stitch across. Count your stitches so that you have the right number of double crochets in each row.

How to Do a Reverse Single Crochet (rsc):

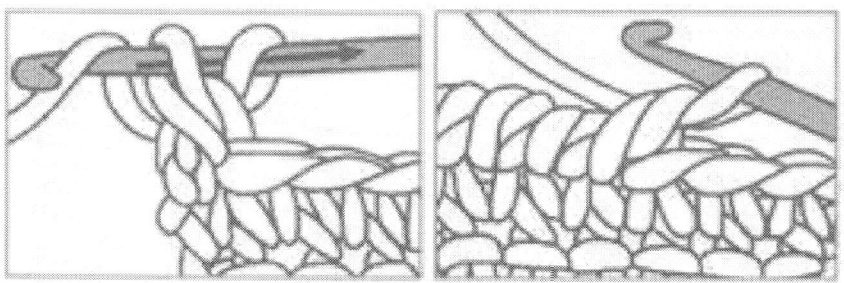

This step is very much like a regular single crochet, except that it's done backwards.

To do this, start by inserting the hook from front to back in the next stitch to the right. Then, pull the yarn over and draw it through the stitch. Bring the yarn over and draw it through the two loops on the hook.

How to Do a Treble Crochet (tc):

Make a chain of 15. Wrap the yarn around the crochet hook from back to front twice, skip the first four chains and then insert the hook into the fifth chain from the hook. Bring the yarn over the crochet hook from back to front and draw it through the chain stitch and on to the working area of the hook. You have four loops on the hook. Bring the yarn over the crochet hook and draw it through the first two loops on the hook. You have three loops on the hook. Bring the yarn over the crochet hook again and draw it through the next two loops on the hook. You have two loops on the hook. Bring the yarn over the crochet hook and draw it through the last two loops on the hook. You have now completed a treble crochet. Continue to treble crochet in each of the remaining chains.

To work the next row of treble crochet, turn your work so that you are working on the back. Do a chain 4, which is called your turning chain. This turning chain is now your first treble crochet of the next row. So start working in the second stitch onwards. Continue to do a treble crochet in each remaining stitch across. Count your stitches so that you have the right number of treble crochets in each row.

Ten Steps to Do the Magic Ring (MR):

The Magic Ring is also called the Magic Circle and is used mainly in amigurumi projects. You continue to work in rounds to achieve a hollow structure that can be stuffed.

Begin by forming a circle with your yarn. Pinch and hold the yarn together where they cross. Insert hook and pull yarn through your ring. Pull the loop all the way through, and up to the top of the ring. Chain 1 and do as many single crochets as required by the pattern. Pull the yarn end and seal the circle.

1.

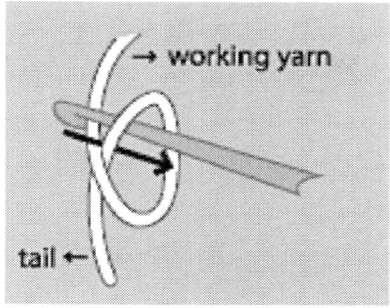

2.

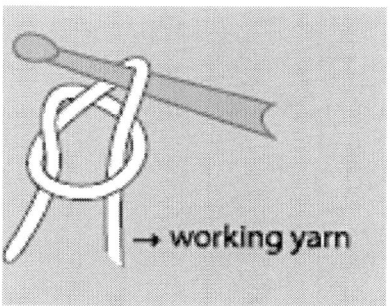

3.

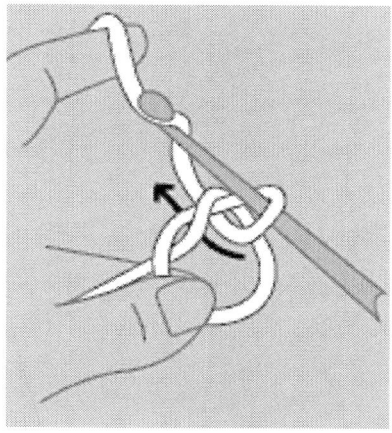

4.

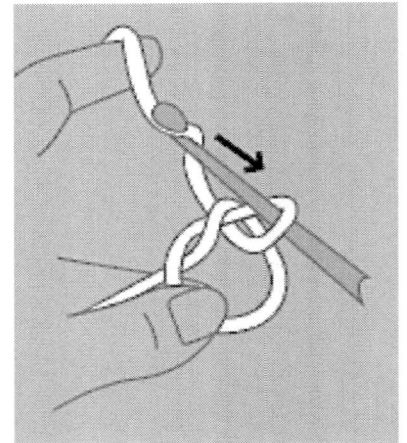

5.

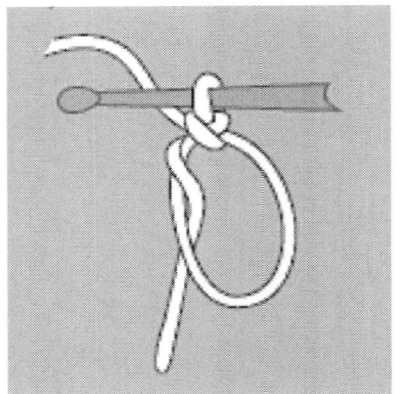

6.

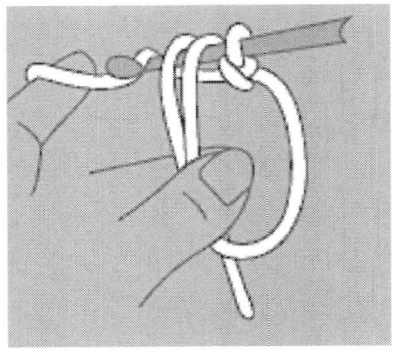

7.

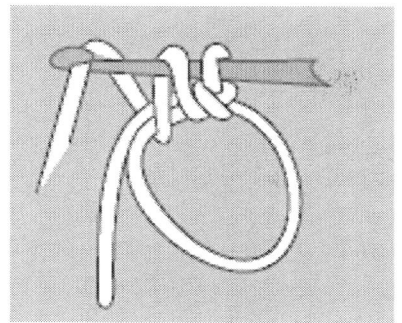

8.

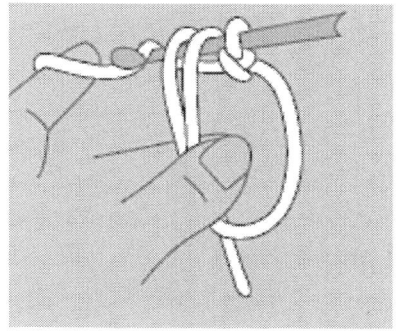

9.

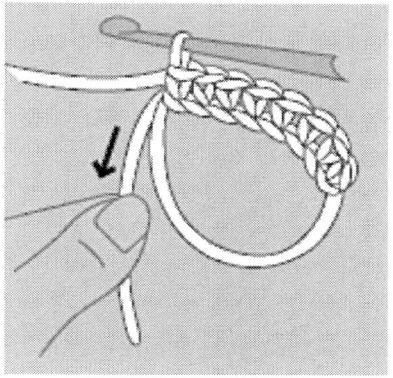

10.

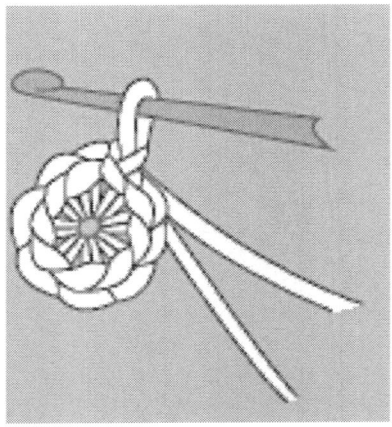

Working in Back Loop Only (BLO)

You can also crochet only in the back loop of a stitch as opposed to both the loops. Insert your crochet hook underneath the back loop only and make a crochet stitch according to your pattern.

Working in Front Loop Only (FLO)

You can also crochet only in the front loop of a stitch as opposed to both the loops. Insert your crochet hook underneath the front loop only and make a crochet stitch according to your pattern.

Increase (inc)

You can increase the number of stitches in a row by repeating the same stitch according to your pattern. So an inc 1 in a row of sc would mean doing two single crochet stitches in the same space.

Decrease (dec)

To decrease the number of stitches in a single crochet row, you can use the sc decrease stitch. Insert the hook into the first stitch, bring the yarn over and draw through the loop. Do not complete the stitch, but insert the hook into the next stitch. Bring the yarn over and draw through the loop. There should be three loops on your hook. Pull the yarn over and draw through all three loops on the hook. This creates a single crochet in the place of two single crochets of the previous row.

What You Need for Amigurumi

1. Yarn: You can use any kind of yarn for amigurumi and that's what makes it easy for most crocheters. You will find three kinds of yarn to be most popular though. They include:
- 100% cotton: This is perfect for people who may be allergic to wool. It also gives a smoother finish to the product.
- Blended yarn: This is a lightweight yarn that is perfect for large projects.
- Acrylic yarn: This is the most economical yarn to work with. It is a fibrous yarn so your stitches need to be tight to keep the product in shape.
2. Crochet hook: Amigurumi projects require the crochet hook to be of a smaller gauge so that the stuffing does not show through. Each pattern will provide you with information about the exact hook size to use. Ideally, the crochet hook size should match with the yarn used.
3. Stuffing: Polyfill stuffing is easily available online and is used to stuff the parts of your toy.
4. Safety eyes/ Beads/ Googly eyes: To accentuate your toy, you can use safety eyes in various sizes. For toys that will be played with by smaller children, it is advisable to sew beads on the toys so they cannot come off easily. Googly eyes are another option that can be glued to the toy. Safety precautions need to be taken in all these cases.
5. Pipe cleaners/Wire: You may need these to give your toy structure and movability.
6. Scissors: Make sure it is a good, sharp pair of scissors to make clean cuts in the yarn.
7. Dog slicker brush: This item is optional, but it is often used to make fuzzy amigurumi. It can be used to brush

the amigurumi to agitate the fibers to create that brushed fur look!

8. Felt: Felt is usually cut in oval shapes and used for the noses, as well as for the lining of ears, hands and feet. The colors used most often are white, brown, beige and black.

Abbreviations Used in the Book:

R – row

st – stitch

ch – chain

sl st – slip stitch

sc – single crochet

hdc – half double crochet

dc – double crochet

tr – treble crochet

dec – decrease

inc – increase

BLO – in back loops only

FO – fasten off

MR – Magic Ring

CC – change color

( ) – repeat instructions

NOTE: The pieces are all worked in rounds (unless otherwise specified), with each row ending with a sl st to the top of the first st.

Chapter 1: The Sea Animals

Ready to begin your amigurumi journey with us? Let's dive into the sea for now. You will absolutely love making these gorgeous sea creatures with their vibrant colors. From a turtle to a whale, we have it all. Using the easy-to- read patterns, you can whip up these beauties in no time. These huggable crochet toys are perfect as gifts or just to adorn your living space.

Dreamy the Starfish

This cute little starfish is waiting to be played with. You can create him in any color you use. This starfish is made by joining two pieces together and stuffing the whole. Sew a smile on his face and let him brighten up your day.

What You Need:

- DK/ worsted yarn in color of your choice 50g
- Black yarn
- 3 mm and 3.5 mm crochet hook
- Stuffing
- Embroidery needle to sew

Body (Make 2)

Using a 3.5 mm hook

R1: 5 sc in MR (5)

R2: 2 sc in each st (10)

R3: (sc 1, inc 1)*5 (15)

R4: (sc 2, inc 1)*5 (20)

R5: (sc 3, inc 1)*5 (25)

Now change to a 3 mm hook

R6: (Ch 14, sl st into the 2nd ch from hook, sl st, 2 sc, 4 hdc, 4 dc, 1 tr, sl st in the next 4 sts of the body) * 5

R7: (1 tr in the first st on the arm, 4 dc, 4 hdc, 2 sc, 2 sl st, continue to sl st in the sts of R6 till you reach the next arm) * 5 [Figures below]

Do not FO.

Assembly

Keeping the two pieces together, sl st around the edges while stuffing as you go.

Using black yarn, embroider eyes and mouth.

Twirl the Octopus

Twirl is a cute little octopus that you can complete in no time. A stuffed body and simple tentacles—this pattern couldn't have been easier. Choose any color you like and make her as bright as possible.

What You Need:

- DK/ worsted yarn in color of your choice 50g
- Scraps of white yarn
- Black yarn
- 3.5 mm crochet hook
- A pair of 6 mm safety eyes
- Stuffing

- Embroidery needle to sew

Body

Use yarn color of your choice

R1: 6 sc in MR (6)

R2: inc in each st (12)

R3: (sc1, inc 1) *6 (18)

R4: (sc 2, inc 1) *6 (24)

R5: (sc 3, inc 1) *6 (30)

R6: (sc 4, inc 1) *6 (36)

R7: (sc 5, inc 1) *6 (42)

R8–13: sc in each st (42)

R14: (sc 5, dec 1) *6 (36)

R15: (sc 4, dec 1) *6 (30)

You can now attach the eyes between R12 and R13 with 8 sts in between. Using black yarn, sew a mouth on R14.

R16: (sc 3, dec 1) *6 (24)

R17: (sc 2, dec 1)*6 (18)

Stuff the body.

R18: (sc 1, dec 1) *6 (12)

R19: dec in each st (6)

FO leaving a long tail to sew.

Tentacles (Make 8)

This is made with two pieces sewn together: one in the main color and one in white.

With white yarn:

R1: Ch 20, turn

R2: sc in 2nd ch from hook, sc in next, hdc in 17 sts FO.

Repeat the same with yarn in main color but do not FO. Keep the pieces together and then sc in 18, 3 sc, sc in 18. Leave a long tail to sew.

Assembly

Sew the tentacles on the head around R5.

Gillian the Jellyfish

A variation of the octopus pattern, this jellyfish will be another cool addition to your collection. Make many of them in various colors. They are absolutely cute and can be used as keychains, as well.

What You Need:

- DK/ worsted yarn in color of your choice 50g
- Black yarn
- 3.5 mm crochet hook
- A pair of 9 mm safety eyes
- Stuffing
- Embroidery needle to sew

Body

Use yarn color of your choice

R1: 6 sc in MR (6)

R2: inc in each st (12)

R3: (sc 1, inc 1) *6 (18)

R4: (sc 2, inc 1) *6 (24)

R5: (sc 3, inc 1) *6 (30)

R6: (sc 4, inc 1) *6 (36)

R7: (sc 5, inc 1) *6 (42)

R8–13: sc in each st (42)

R14: BLO (sc 5, dec 1) * 6 (36)

R15: (sc 4, dec 1) * 6 (30)

You can now attach the eyes between R12 and R13 with 8 sts in between.

Using black yarn sew a mouth on R14.

R16: (sc 3, dec 1) *6 (24)

R17: (sc 2, dec 1) *6 (18)

Stuff the body.

R18: (sc 1 , dec 1) *6 (12)

R19: dec in each st (6)

FO leaving a long tail to sew.

Skirt

Using the front loops of R14, attach yarn to any of the sts.

Ch 3, 2 dc in the same st, skip 1 sc, sc in the next, (skip 1 sc, 5 dc in next sc, skip 1 sc, sc in next) * repeat around, 2 dc in first st, sl st to top of ch 3.

FO.

Tentacles (Make 3)

Ch 31, 2 sc in 2nd ch from hook, 3 sc in every remaining st. FO leaving a long tail to sew.

Assembly

Sew the tentacles to the center of the body base.

Wally the Whale

Wally is a tiny whale with a large heart! This quick-to-make pattern will have you creating several of them in no time. Attach safety eyes or glue on googly eyes for that impressive look. Choose colors of your choice to make Wally the Whale.

What You Need:

- DK/worsted yarn in blue and white
- 3.5 mm crochet hook
- A pair of 9 mm safety eyes
- Stuffing
- Embroidery needle to sew

Body

Use blue yarn

R1: 6 sc in MR (6)

R2: inc in each st (12)

R3: (sc 1, inc 1) *6 (18)

R4: (sc 2, inc 1) *6 (24)

R5: (sc 3, inc 1) *6 (30)

R6: (sc 4, inc 1) *6 (36)

R7: (sc 5, inc 1) *6 (42)

R8: (sc 6,inc 1) *6 (48)

R9: (sc 7, inc 1) *6 (54)

R10–20: sc in each (54)

R21: (sc 7, dec 1) * 6 (48)

Change to white yarn.

R22: sc in each st (48)

R23: (sc 4, dec 1) *8 (40)

R24: (sc 2, dec 1) *8 (30)

R25: (sc 1, dec 1) *8 (20)

Stuff the body.

R26: dec in all st (10)

R27: dec in all st (5)

FO.

Fins (Make 2)

Use blue yarn.

R1: 6 sc in MR (6)

R2: inc in each st (12)

R3–6: sc in each st (12)

Fold and sc across to close the gap.

FO leaving a long tail to sew.

Sew the fins to the side of the body at R27.

Tail

Use blue yarn.

Make 2

R1: 6 sc in MR (6)

R2: inc in each st (12)

R3–6: sc in each st (12)

Fold and sc across to close the gap.

FO

Join the two tail pieces at the R1 edge to form a V shape tail. Sew this tail to the body at R27.

Billy the Turtle

Another cute pattern that kids will love! Billy is simple enough to create and can be either made with a single color or multiple colors. Billy is small in size but packs a punch. You can make him larger in size by just using larger size hooks.

What You Need:

- DK/ worsted yarn in colors of your choice (B for color1, W for color2)
- 3.5 mm crochet hook
- A pair of 9 mm safety eyes
- Stuffing
- Embroidery needle to sew

Body

Use B.

R1: 6 sc in MR (6)

Change to W.

R2: inc in each st (12)

Change to B.

R3: (sc 1, inc 1) * 6 (18)

Change to W.

R4: sc in each st (18)

Change to B.

R5: (sc 2, inc 1) * 6 (24)

Change to W.

R6: sc in each st (24)

Change to B.

R7: (sc 3, inc 1) * 6 (30)

Change to W.

R8: sc in each st (30)

Change to B.

R9: sc in each st (30)

Change to W.

R10: sc in each st (30)

R11: BLO (sc 3, dec 1) * 6 (24)

R12: (sc 2, dec 1) * 6 (18)

Stuff the body.

R13: (sc 1, dec 1) * 6 (12)

R14: dec in each st (6)

Fasten off and weave in the ends.

Head

Use white yarn.

R1: 6 sc in MR (6)

R2: inc in each st (12)

R3: (sc 1, inc 1) *6 (18)

R4: (sc 2, inc 1) *6 (24)

R5–7: sc in each st (24)

R8: (sc 2, dec 1) * 6 (18)

Attach the eyes at R6.

R9: sc in each st (18)

R10: (sc 1, dec 1) * 6 (12)

FO leaving a long tail to sew.

Stuff the head and sew it to the body.

Legs (Make 4)

Use white yarn.

R1: 6 sc in MR (6)

R2–3: sc in each st (6)

FO leaving a long tail to sew. Sew the legs to the body at R11.

Tail

Use white yarn.

Ch4, sl st in 2nd ch from hook, sl st, sc.

FO leaving a long tail to sew.

Sew the tail to the body at R11.

Cheri the Crab

Cheri is a chubby little crab all ready to play with you. Make her in any color you like but red is her favorite. The pattern is a very simple one with a little bit of work on the claws. Try out this amigurumi pattern today.

What You Need:

- DK/ worsted yarn in color of your choice
- 3.5 mm crochet hook
- A pair of 6mm safety eyes
- Stuffing
- Embroidery needle to sew

Body

R1: 6 sc in MR (6)

R2: inc in each st (12)

R3: (sc 1, inc 1) *6 (18)

R4: (sc 2, inc 1) *6 (24)

R5: (sc 3, inc 1) *6 (30)

R6: (sc 4, inc 1) *6 (36)

R7–8: sc in each st (36)

R9: (sc 4, dec 1) * 6 (30)

R10: (sc 3, dec 1) * 6 (24)

R11: (sc 2, dec 1) * 6 (18)

R12: (sc 1, dec 1) * 6 (12)

R13: dec * 6 (6)

Stuff the body.

Fasten off and weave in the ends.

Legs (Make 4-6)

R1: 5 sc in MR (5)

R2–7: sc in each st (5)

FO leaving a long tail to sew. Sew the legs to the body.

Claws (Make 2)

R1: 4 sc in MR (4)

R2: (sc 1, inc 1) * 2 (6)

R3: (sc 2, inc 1) * 2 (8)

R4: sc in each st (8)

R5: (sc 3, inc 1) * 2 (10)

R6: Ch 3, sc in the 2nd ch from hook, sc in next st, now working on the sts of R5—sc in each st ending with an sc under the triangular piece just made.

R7: sc 5, dec 1, sc 4 (10)

R8: sc 5, dec 1, sc 3 (9)

R9: dec 1, sc 3, dec 1, sc 2 (7)

R10: dec 1, sc 2, dec 1, sc 1 (5)

R11–14: sc in each st (5)

FO leaving a long tail to sew.

Sew the claws on the body. Sew eyes on the body at R7.

Kate the Clown Fish

Doesn't Kate look adorable?? Grab your supplies and let's get started on this funny little clownfish. With bright orange and white yarn and bulging eyes, Kate is all set to impress you. This is an easy pattern to follow that includes color changing.

What You Need:

- DK/ worsted yarn in orange, white and black
- 3.5 mm crochet hook
- A pair of 6mm safety eyes
- Stuffing
- Embroidery needle to sew

Body

Use orange yarn.

R1: 6 sc in MR (6)

R2: inc in each st (12)

R3: (sc 1, inc 1) * 6 (18)

R4: (sc 2, inc 1) * 6 (24)

R5: (sc 3, inc 1) * 6 (30)

R6–7: sc in each st (30)

R8: (sc 4, inc 1) * 6 (36)

Change to black yarn.

Place eyes at R4 with 5 sts in between.

R9: sc in each st (36)

Change to white yarn.

R10–11: sc in each st (36)

Change to black yarn.

R12: sc in each st (36)

Change to orange yarn.

R13: sc in each st (36)

R14: (sc 4, dec 1)*6 (30)

R15–16: sc in each st (30)

Change to black.

R17: sc in each st (30)

Change to white.

R18: (sc 3, dec 1) *6 (24)

Change to black.

R19: sc in each st (24)

Change to orange yarn.

R20: sc in each st (24)

R21: (sc 2, dec 1) * 6 (18)

R22: sc in each st (18)

Change to black yarn.

R23: sc in each st (18)

Change to white.

R24: sc in each st (18)

R25: (sc 1, dec 1) *6 (12)

R26: dec * 6 (6)

Fasten off and weave in the ends.

Fins (Make 3)

Use orange yarn.

R1: Ch 7, sc in 2nd ch from hook, sc in next 5 st

R2: Turn, ch1, sc in each st

R3: Turn, ch1, sc in first 2 st, dec 1, sc in last 2 sts

R4–5: Turn, ch1, sc in each st

R6: Turn, ch1, dec 1, sc 1, dec 1

FO leaving a long tail to sew.

Attach one fin to each side of the body at R12. Attach the third fin to the back of the body.

Dorsal Fin

Use orange yarn.

R1: Ch10, sc in 2nd ch from hook, sc in next 8 st

R2: Turn, ch1, sc, hdc, dc, hdc, sc, sc, hdc, hdc, sc

R3: Turn, ch1, sc, hdc, hdc, sc, sc, hdc, dc, hdc, sc

R4: sc, sc

FO leaving a long tail to sew.

Attach the fin to the top of the body.

Eyes (Make 2)

Use white yarn.

R1: 6sc in MR (6)

R2: inc in each st (12)

R3: (sc 1, inc 1) * 6 (18)

FO leaving a long tail to sew.

With the wrong side facing out, attach the safety eyes, one inside of each crocheted eye, and sew in place on the body.

Sew a mouth using black yarn below the eyes.

Chapter 2: The Home Buddies

Now let's crochet some of our much loved pets! These home buddies are perfect animals to crochet especially for kids. With cute faces, they represent the love that pets have for us. Create them in vibrant colors and see your child's face light up in awe. Let's make all of them now!

Cleo the Chic

Let Cleo the Chick dazzle you with her sparkling eyes. This little chick is perfect for Easter, too, as a holiday gift. With simple stitches you can ruffle up Cleo in no time. Make her in different colors to attract the young ones.

What You Need:

- DK/ worsted yarn in color of your choice
- Orange yarn
- 4 mm crochet hook
- A pair of 6 mm safety eyes
- Stuffing
- Embroidery needle to sew

Body

R1: 6 sc in MR (6)

R2: inc in each st (12)

R3: (sc 1, inc 1) * 6 (18)

R4: (sc 5, inc 1) * 3 (21)

R5: (sc 6, inc 1) * 3 (24)

R6: (sc 7, inc 1) * 3 (27)

R7: (sc 8, inc 1) * 3 (30)

R8: (sc 9, inc 1) * 3 (33)

R9: (sc 10, inc 1) *3 (36)

R10–17: sc in each st (36)

Stuff the body.

Attach eyes at R10.

R18: (sc 4, dec 1) * 6 (30)

R19: (sc 3, dec 1) *6 (24)

R20: (sc 2, dec 1) *6 (18)

R21: (sc 1, dec 1) *6 (12)

R22: dec 1 * 6 (6)

Fasten off and weave in the ends.

Cut four pieces of yarn about inches long and attach to the top of the head with a knot. Trim the length accordingly.

Wings (Make 2)

R1: 5 sc in MR (5)

R2: Ch1, turn, sc in 1st sc, 2 hdc, 3 dc, 2 hdc, slst

R3: Ch1, turn, sc, sc, sc, inc 1, inc 1, inc 1, sc, sc, sc

FO leaving a long tail to sew.

Sew the top of the wings on the side of the body at R11.

Beak

Use orange yarn to embroider straight stitches around R12 and R13 between the eyes.

Feet

Use orange yarn.

[Ch5, sl st in 2nd ch from hook, (ch2,sl st in each of these 2ch) *2, sl st in remaining 3 ch] * 2

FO leaving a long tail to sew.

Sew the feet to the bottom of the body towards the front.

Mike the Mouse

A mouse around the house can be fun, too. Let those adoring eyes draw you towards him. Mike is super quick to create and can be made in a variety of colors. Change the crochet hook size to create larger versions of him.

What You Need:

- DK/ worsted yarn in color of your choice
- Pink yarn
- 3 mm and 3.5 mm crochet hook
- A pair of 4 mm safety eyes
- Stuffing
- Embroidery needle to sew

Body

Use 3.5 mm hook

R1: Ch2, 4 sc in 2nd ch from hook (4)

R2: (inc 1, sc 1) *2 (6)

R3: (sc 1, inc 1) *3 (9)

R4: (sc 2, inc 1) *3 (12)

R5: sc in each st (12)

R6: (sc 2, inc 1)*4 (16)

R7: (sc 3, inc 1) *4 (20)

Attach eyes at R4 with 5 stitches in between.

R8–13: sc in each st (20)

R14: (sc 3, dec 1) * 4 (16

Stuff the body.

R15: (sc 2, dec 1) * 4 (12)

R16: dec in each st (6)

R17: (skip next st, sl st) * 3 (3)

R18: Ch 20

Fasten off and weave in the ends.

Ears (Make 2)

Use 3 mm hook

R1: 6 sc in MR (6)

R2: inc in each st (12)

FO leaving a long tail to sew.

Sew the ears at R10.

Using pink yarn, embroider around R1 of the body to look like a nose.

Tuffy the Dog

Now who doesn't want their favorite pet as a toy? For those who cannot keep the real ones at home, this is the best option. So make this cuddly dog and have fun playing with him for years. With his cute tongue sticking out, he will be a great companion all day long.

What You Need:

- DK/ worsted yarn in color of your choice
- Red yarn
- 3.5 mm crochet hook
- A pair of 4 mm safety eyes
- Stuffing
- Embroidery needle to sew

Head

R1: 6 sc in MR (6)

R2: inc in each st (12)

R3: (sc 1, inc 1) * 6 (18)

R4: (sc 2, inc 1) * 6 (24)

R5–9: sc in each st (24)

R10: (sc 3, inc 1) * 6 (30)

R11: (sc 4, inc 1) * 6 (36)

R12: (sc 5, inc 1) * 5, sc 6 (41)

R13: (sc 6, inc 1) * 5, sc 6 (46)

R14: (sc 7, inc 1) * 5, sc 6 (51)

R15–17: sc in each st (51)

R18: (sc 7, dec 1) * 5, sc 6 (46)

R19: (sc 6, dec 1) * 5, sc 6 (41)

R20: (sc 5, dec 1) * 5, sc 6 (36)

R21: sc in each st (36)

R22: (sc 4, dec 1) *6 (30)

R23: (sc 3, dec 1) *6 (24)

R24: (sc 2, dec 1) *6 (18)

Attach safety eyes in place. Stuff the head.

R25: (sc 1, dec 1) * 6 (12)

R26: dec * 6 (6)

Fasten off and weave in the ends.

Using black yarn, sew a nose with straight stitches.

Ears (Make 2)

R1: 3 sc in MR (3)

R2: inc in each st (6)

R3: (sc 1, inc 1) * 3 (9)

R4: sc in each st (9)

R5: (sc 2, inc 1) * 3 (12)

R6: sc in each st (12)

R7: (sc 3, inc 1) * 3 (15)

R8: sc in each st (15)

R9: (sc 4, inc 1) * 3 (18)

R10–16: sc in each st (18)

Sew the open ends using sc. FO leaving a long tail to sew. Sew the ears to the side of the head.

Body

R1: 8 sc in MR (8)

R2: inc in each st (16)

R3: (sc 1, inc 1) * 8 (24)

R4: (sc 2, inc 1) * 8 (32)

R5: (sc 3, inc 1) * 8 (40)

R6–17: sc in each st (40)

R18: (sc 3, dec 1)*8 (32)

R19–25: sc in each st (32)

R26: (sc 2, dec 1) * 8 (24)

R27: (sc 1, dec 1) * 8 (16)

Stuff the body.

R28: dec * 8 (8)

FO leaving a long tail to sew.

Attach the head to the body.

Legs (Make 4)

R1: 6 sc in MR (6)

R2: inc in each st (12)

R3: (sc 1, inc 1) * 6 (18)

R4: (sc 2, inc 1) * 6 (24)

R5–6: sc in each st (24)

R7: sc 12, (sc 2, dec 1) * 3 (21)

R8: sc 12, (sc 1, dec 1) * 3 (18)

R9: sc 12, (dec 1) * 3 (15)

R10–21: sc in each st (15)

Stuff the legs and FO leaving a long tail to sew.

Sew the legs closed and sew in place on the body.

Tail

Ch 10, sc in 2nd ch from hook, sc, sc, hdc in 6 sts.

FO and sew the tail to the body.

Tongue

Use red yarn

R1:Ch 4, sc in 2nd ch from hook, sc , sc R2: Ch1, turn, inc 1, sc, inc 1

R3: Ch1, turn, sc in each st

R4: Ch1, turn, dec 1, sc, dec 1

FO and sew to the muffle.

Snips the Bunny

Snips is such an adorable little bunny that you would love to keep around the house. With perfect long ears he is a unique gift for everyone. You can make Snips colorful, too. Just run wild with your imagination and you could have a whole family of bunnies ready to play with.

What You Need:

- DK/ worsted yarn in color of your choice
- 4 mm crochet hook

- A pair of 6 mm safety eyes
- Stuffing
- Embroidery needle to sew

Head & Body

R1: 6 sc in MR (6)

R2: inc in each st (12)

R3: (sc 1, inc 1) *6 (18)

R4: (sc 2, inc 1) *6 (24)

R5: (sc 3, inc 1) *6 (30)

R6: (sc 4, inc 1) *6 (36)

R7: (sc 5, inc 1) *6 (42)

R8–14: sc in each st (42)

Attach safety eyes at R11.

R15: (sc 5, dec 1) *6 (36)

R16: (sc 4, dec 1) *6 (30)

R17: (sc 3, dec 1) *6 (24)

R18: (sc 2, dec 1) *6 (18)

R19: (sc 1, dec 1) * 6 (12)

Stuff the head and continue working the body.

R20: (sc 5, inc 1) * 2 (14)

R21: (sc 1, inc 1) * 7 (21)

R22: (sc 2, inc 1) * 7 (28)

R23–28: sc in each st (28)

R29: (sc 2, dec 1) *7 (21)

R30: (sc 1, dec 1) *7 (14)

R31: dec * 7 (7)

Stuff the body well.

Fasten off and weave in the ends.

Ears (Make 2)

R1: 5 sc in MR (5)

R2: inc in each st (10)

R3: (sc 1, inc 1) * 5 (15)

R4–5: sc in each st (15)

R6: (sc 3, dec 1) * 3 (12)

R7: sc in each st (12)

R8: (sc 2, dec 1) * 3 (9)

R9: sc in each st (9)

R10: (sc 1, dec 1) *3 (6)

FO leaving a long tail to sew.

Sew the ears to the top of the head.

Arms (Make 2)

R1: 6 sc in MR (6)

R2: (sc 1, inc 1) * 3 (9)

R3: sc in each st (9)

R4: (sc 1, dec 1) * 3 (6)

R5–8: sc in each st

FO leaving a long tail to sew.

Attach the arms to the side of the body.

Legs (Make 2)

R1: 6 sc in MR (6)

R2: inc in each st (12)

R3: (sc 1, inc 1) *6 (18)

R4-6: sc in each st (18)

Stuff the legs.

R7: (sc 1, dec 1) * 6 (12)

R8: dec * 6 (6)

R9: sc in each st (6)

FO leaving a long tail to sew. Attach the legs to the body.

Tail

R1: 6 sc in MR (6)

R2: inc in each st (12)

R3: sc in each st (12)

R4: dec * 6 (6)

FO leaving a long tail to sew. Attach the tail to the body.

Tina the Pusheen Cat

This cartoon cat character is a lovable crochet toy that you can create for your kids. You can change the colors of the yarn to make her attractive. This cuddly toy is perfect for kids who love the Pusheen character. So go ahead and have fun creating this fantastic home buddy.

What You Need:

- DK/ worsted yarn in light grey (L), dark grey (D), black (B)
- 4 mm crochet hook
- A pair of 6 mm safety eyes
- Stuffing
- Embroidery needle to sew

Body

Use L

R1: 6 sc in MR (6)

R2: sc inc in each st (12)

R3: (sc in 1 st, sc inc 1) * 6 (18)

R4: (sc in 2 sts, sc inc 1) *6 (24)

R5: (sc in 3 sts, sc inc 1) *6 (30)

R6: (sc in 4 sts, sc inc 1) *6 (36)

R7: sc in 3 sts, CC D sc in 9 sts, CC L sc in 24 sts (36)

R8: sc in 3 sts, CC D sc in 10 sts, CC L sc in 23 sts (36)

R9–10: sc in each st (36)

R11: sc in 3 sts, CC D sc in 11 sts, CC L sc in 22 sts (36)

R12: sc in 3 sts, CC D sc in 12 sts, CC L sc in 21 sts (36)

R13–19: sc in each st (36)

Attach safety eyes.

R20: (sc in 4 sts, sc dec 1) * 6 (30)

R21: (sc in 3 sts, sc dec 1) * 6 (24)

R22: (sc in 2 sts, sc dec 1) * 6 (18)

R23: (sc in 1 st, sc dec 1) * 6 (12)

Stuff the head and continue working the body R24: (dec) * 6 (6)

Fasten off and weave in the ends.

Tail

Use D

R1: 6 sc in MR (6)

R2: (sc in 1 st, sc inc 1) * 3 (9)

CC L

R3–4: sc in each st (9)

CC D

R5–6: sc in each st (9)

CC L

R7–8: sc in each st (9)

CC D

R9: sc in each st (9)

Stuff the tail.

R10: (sc in 1 sts, sc dec 1) *3 (6)

Fasten off leaving a long tail to sew.

Attach the tail to the body.

Ears (Make 2)

Use L

R1: 3 sc in MR (3)

R2: sc inc in each st (6)

R3: sc in each st (6)

R4: (sc in 1 st, sc inc 1) * 3 (9)

Fasten off leaving a long tail to sew.

Attach the ears to the top of the body.

Feet (Make 4)

Use L

R1: 3 sc in MR (3)

R2: sc inc in each st (6)

Fasten off leaving a long tail to sew.

Attach the feet to the bottom of the body.

Using B embroider a mouth and whiskers.

Sew three straight stitches above the eyes with D.

Chapter 3: The Farm Animals

Here are some of the cutest farm animals that you will surely enjoy crocheting. From a pig to a cow or a sheep to an alpaca, we have a nice collection here. Make them in different sizes and have an assortment of barn animals. These incredible patterns are simple to create. Add your choice of yarn colors and choose from types of soft and snuggly yarn to make it personal.

Sheila the Sheep

How cute is Sheila the Sheep?! You may choose to sew it in one color or two, and if you want to increase its size just use a bigger hook size.

What You Need:

- DK/ worsted yarn in Black and White
- 3.5 mm crochet hook

- A pair of 6 mm safety eyes
- Stuffing
- Embroidery needle to sew

Body

Use white yarn.

R1: 6 sc in MR (6)

R2: inc in each st (12)

R3: (sc 1, inc 1) *6 (18)

R4: (sc 2, inc 1) *6 (24)

R5: (sc 3, inc 1) *6 (30)

R6: (sc 4, inc1) *6 (36)

R7–12: sc in each st (36)

R13: (sc 4, dec 1) *6 (30)

R14: (sc 3, dec 1) *6 (24)

R15: (sc 2, dec 1) *6 (18)

Stuff the body.

R16: (sc 1 ,dec 1) *6 (12)

R17: dec * 6 (6)

Fasten off and weave in the ends.

Head

Use black yarn.

R1: 6 sc in MR (6)

R2: inc in each st (12)

R3: (sc 1, inc 1) * 6 (18)

R4: (sc 2, inc 1) * 6 (24)

R5–7: sc in each st (24)

R8: (sc 2, dec 1) * 6 (18)

Stuff the head.

R9: (sc 1, dec 1) * 6 (12)

R11: (dec 1) * 6 (6)

Fasten off and weave in the ends.

Legs (Make 4)

Use black yarn

R1: 6 sc in MR (6)

R2: inc in each st (12)

R3–5: sc in each st (12)

Stuff the legs and sew them to the body.

Tail

Use black yarn

R1: 6 sc in MR (6)

R2: inc in each st (12)

R3: (sc 1, inc 1) * 6 (18)

Stuff the tail and sew to the body.

Ears (Make 2)

Use black yarn.

R1: 6 sc in MR (6)

R2: inc in each st (12)

FO leaving a long tail to sew.

Sew the ears to the body.

Paulie the Pig

A farm won't be complete without Paulie the Pig. I chose the pink color but you can choose whatever color you like to add to your farm collection.

What You Need:

- DK/ worsted yarn in pink or color of your choice 50g
- Black yarn
- 3.5 mm crochet hook
- A pair of 6 mm safety eyes
- Stuffing
- Embroidery needle to sew

Head & Body

R1: 6 sc in MR (6)

R2: (inc 1, sc 1) * 3 (9)

R3: (BLO) sc in each st (9)

R4: sc in each st (9)

R5: (inc 1, sc 2) *3 (12)

R6: sc in each st (12)

R7: (inc 1, sc 1) *6 (18)

R8: (inc1, sc2)*6 (24)

R9: (inc1, sc3)*6 (30)

R10: (inc 1, sc 9) * 3 (33)

You can now attach safety eyes between R7 and R8 with 6 sts in between.

R11–19: sc in each st (33)

R20: (dec 1, sc 9) * 3 (30)

R21: (dec 1, sc 3) * 6 (24)

Stuff the pig now and continue stuffing as you go.

R22: (dec 1, sc 2) * 6 (18)

R23: (dec 1, sc 1) * 6 (12)

R24: dec * 6 (6)

Stuff well. Fasten off and weave in the ends.

Tail

Chain 20.

Sl st in the second ch from hook and in the remaining 18 chains. FO leaving a long tail for sewing.

Attach the tail to the body at the center of R24.

Legs (Make 4)

R1: 6 sc in MR (6)

R2–3: sc in each st (6)

Sl st in next st.

FO leaving a long tail for sewing. Stuff the leg.

Once you create all 4 legs, sew on the two legs at R9 with 4 sts in between the two legs at R14 with 6 sts in between.

Ears (Make 2)

R1: 3 sc in MR, ch1, Turn (3)

R2: 2 sc in each of the 3 sts (6)

R3: 2 sc in MR (8)

FO leaving a long tail for sewing.

Sew the ears at R9 with 4 sts in between.

Finishing

Using black yarn, make small straight stitches for nostrils at R2.

Pru the Alpaca

Here is a cute alpaca with soft fuzzy hair that you can play with. This is one adorable animal from South America. Add muted colors for Pru and you have the best cuddly toy/animal collection around.

What You Need:

- DK/ worsted yarn in color of your choice
- 3.5 mm crochet hook
- A pair of 4 mm safety eyes
- Stuffing
- Embroidery needle to sew

Body

R1: 8 sc in MR (8)

R2: inc in each st (16)

R3: (sc in 1 st, sc inc 1) * 8 (24)

R4: (sc in 2 sts, sc in c 1) *8 (32)

R5: (sc in 3 sts, sc in c1) *8 (40)

R6–26: sc in each st (40)

R27: (sc in 3 sts, sc dec 1) * 8 (32)

R28: (sc in 2 sts, sc dec 1) * 8 (24)

R29: (sc in 1 st, sc dec 1) * 8 (16)

Stuff the body

R30: sc dec * 8 (8)

Fasten off and weave in the ends.

Head

R1: 8 sc in MR (8)

R2: inc in each st (16)

R3: (sc in 1 st, sc inc 1) * 8 (24)

R4: (sc in 2 sts, sc inc 1) * 8 (32)

R5–14: sc in each st (32)

Attach safety eyes at R7

R16: (sc in 2 sts, sc dec 1) *8 (24)

R17–27: sc in each st (24)

R28: (sc in 1 st, sc dec 1) *8 (16)

Stuff the head

FO leaving a long tail to sew.

Attach the head to the body.

Mouth

R1: 6 sc in MR (6)

R2: inc in each st (12)

R3: (sc in 1 st, sc inc 1) * 6 (18)

R4–5: sc in each st (18)

Stuff the mouth.

FO leaving a long tail to sew.

Attach the mouth to the head.

Legs (Make 4)

R1: 6 sc in MR (6)

R2: inc in each st (12)

R3: (sc in 1 st, sc inc 1) * 6 (18)

R4–10: sc in each st (18)

R11: (sc in 2 sts, sc inc 1) *6 (24)

R12: sc in each st (24)

Stuff the legs.

FO leaving a long tail to sew.

Attach the legs to the body.

Ears (Make 2)

R1: 3 sc in MR (3)

R2: inc in each st (6)

R3–5: sc in each st (6)

FO leaving a long tail to sew.

Attach the ears to the head.

For the hair, cut four pieces of yarn 4 inches in length and attach to the front of the head in a knot. Open up each strand of yarn to give a fluffier look.

For the tail, cut four pieces of yarn 4 inches in length and attach to the back of the body in a knot. Open up each strand of yarn to give a fluffier look.

Dina the Duck

Dina is a colorful duck all ready to mingle with you. Play with different colors to achieve an attractive toy. This little duck is all set to say "quack quack quack."

What You Need:

- DK/ worsted yarn in colors of your choice
- 3 mm crochet hook
- A pair of 4 mm safety eyes
- Stuffing
- Embroidery needle to sew

Head

R1: 6 sc in MR (6)

R2: sc inc in each st (12)

R3: (sc in 1 st, sc inc 1) * 6 (18)

R4: (sc in 2 sts, sc inc 1) * 6 (24)

R5: (sc in 3 sts, sc inc 1) * 6 (30)

R6: (sc in 4 sts, sc inc 1) * 6 (36)

R7: (sc in 5 sts, sc inc 1) * 6 (42)

R8: (sc in 6 sts, sc inc 1) * 6 (48)

R9–19: sc in each st (48)

Attach eyes at R14 with 8 sts in between.

R20: (sc in 6 sts, sc dec 1) *6 (42)

R21: (sc in 5 sts, sc dec 1) *6 (36)

R22: (sc in 4 sts, sc dec 1) *6 (30)

R23: (sc in 3 sts, sc dec 1) *6 (24)

R24: (sc in 2 sts, sc dec 1) *6 (18)

R25: (sc in 1 st, sc dec 1) * 6 (12)

R26: (sc dec) * 6 (6)

Stuff the head.

Fasten and weave in the ends.

Body

R1: 6 sc in MR (6)

R2: sc inc in each st (12)

R3: (sc in 1 st, sc inc 1) * 6 (18)

R4: (sc in 2 sts, sc inc 1) *6 (24)

R5: (sc in 3 sts, sc inc 1) *6 (30)

R6: (sc in 4 sts, sc inc 1)*6 (36)

R7–10: sc in each st (36)

R11: (sc in 4 sts, sc dec 1) *6 (30)

R12–13: sc in each st (30)

R14: (sc in 3 sts, sc dec 1) *6 (24)

R15–17: sc in each st (24)

R18: (sc in 2 sts, sc dec 1) *6 (18)

Stuff the body.

FO leaving a long tail to sew.

Wings (Make 2)

R1: 6 sc into MR (6)

R2: sc in each st (6)

R3: inc in each st (12)

R4–9: sc in each st (12)

Fold the piece in half and make 6 sc to close.

FO leaving a long tail to sew.

Sew the wings to the side of the body.

Feet (Make 2)

R1: Ch 4

R2: sc in 3 st, ch1, turn (3)

R3: sc inc 1, sc, sc inc 1, ch1, turn (5)

R4: sc inc 1, sc in 3 sts, sc inc 1, ch1, turn (7)

R5: sc inc 1, sc in 5 sts, sc inc 1, ch1, turn (9)

R6: sl st, (hdc, ch1, sl st, sl st) * 2, hdc, ch1, sl st

Fasten off and weave in the ends.

Sew the feet to the bottom of the body.

Beak

R1: ch 5, inc in 2nd ch from hook, sc in 2 sts, 3 sc in next st, now working behind the stitches, sc in 2 sts, sc in 1st st (10)

R2: sc in each st (10)

R3: sc inc 1, sc in 4 sts, sc inc 1, sc in 4 sts (12)

R4: sc, sc inc 1, sc in 5 sts, sc inc 1, sc in 4 sts (14)

R5: sc, sc, sc inc 1, sc in 6 sts, sc inc 1, sc in 4 sts (16)

Stuff the beak lightly.

FO leaving a long tail to sew.

Sew the beak to the front of the head.

Hair

Cut two strands of yarn 3 inches long. Fold each in half and, using a 1.5 mm hook, attach it to the top of the head by making a knot. Put the needle on any of the sc on the first row of the head, pick the yarn and pull out and make a sl st. Trim the yarn to about 1 inch.

Chapter 4: The Wild Ones

The wild animals are some of the most majestic. We give you some simple patterns with which to create these stunning wild animals. You will find the patterns to be similar in nature with a few specific changes here and there. So this is a good collection for you to have as you master the art of amigurumi. Browse through this section to find your favorite wild one and begin the magic of crochet. Your creation will surely be loved by all.

Holly the Hippo

Holly the Hippo is a simple yet fun pattern that you can create easily. With a large head, she demands attention from all around her. Try out various colors of yarn to make her colorful and fun to play with.

What You Need:

- DK/ worsted yarn in color of your choice
- Pink yarn
- 4 mm crochet hook
- A pair of 6mm safety eyes
- Stuffing
- Embroidery needle to sew

Head

Ch 4

R1: 2 sc in 2nd ch from hook, sc, 3 sc in last ch.

Working along the back of the chain, sc, sc (8)

R2: inc 1 in first sc, inc 1, sc, inc 1, inc 1, inc 1, sc, inc 1 (14)

R3: inc 1 in first sc, inc 1, sc in next 4 sc, inc 1, inc 1, inc 1, sc in next 4 sc, inc 1. (20)

R4–7: sc in each sc (20) R8:(dec 1, dec 1, sc in next 6 sc) *2 (16)

R9: (dec 1, sc in next 6 sc) * 2 (14)

R10-11: sc in each st (14)

Stuff the body.

R12: (dec 1, sc 2) * around and end with dec 1 in last 2 sc (10)

R13: dec in each st (5)

Fasten off and weave in the ends.

Body

R1: 5 sc in MR (5)

R2: inc in each st (10)

R3: (sc 1, inc 1) *5 (15)

R4: (sc 2, inc 1) *5 (20)

R5: (sc 3, inc 1) *5 (25)

R6–8: sc in each st (25)

R9: (sc 3, dec 1) * 5 (20)

R10–12: sc in each st (20)

R13: (dec 1, sc 2) * 5 (15)

FO leaving a long tail to sew. Sew head to the body.

Ears (Make 2)

R1: 6 sc in MR (6)

R2: inc in each st (12)

FO leaving a long tail to sew.

Sew ears to head.

Using pink yarn, embroider straight and stitch for nostrils.

Legs (Make 4)

R1: 6 sc in MR (6)

R2–4: sc in each st (6)

FO leaving a long tail to sew. Sew the legs to the body.

Tail

Ch 4, sl st in 2nd ch from hook, sc, sc.

Fasten off and weave in the ends.

Sew tail to body.

Rob the Rhino

This rhino pattern is similar to the hippo pattern given above. With the addition of the horns, the pattern can be changed to that of a rhino. So enjoy this simple pattern and create a range of wild ones.

What You Need:

- DK/ worsted yarn in color of your choice
- Dark Grey yarn
- 4 mm crochet hook
- A pair of 6 mm safety eyes
- Stuffing
- Embroidery needle to sew

Head

Ch 4

R1: 2 sc in 2nd ch from hook, sc, 3 sc in last ch.

Working along the back of the chain, sc, sc (8)

R2: inc 1 in first sc, inc 1, sc, inc 1, inc 1, inc 1, sc, inc 1 (14)

R3: inc 1 in first sc, inc 1, sc in next 4 sc, inc 1, inc 1, inc 1, sc in next 4 sc, inc 1. (20)

R4–7: sc in each sc (20)

R8: (dec 1, dec 1, sc in next 6 sc) *2 (16)

R9: (dec 1, sc in next 6 sc) * 2 (14)

R10–11: sc in each st (14)

Stuff the body.

R12: (dec 1, sc 2) * around and end with dec 1 in last 2 sc (10)

R13: dec in each st (5)

Fasten off and weave in the ends.

Horns

Use dark grey yarn

SMALL

R1: 3 sc in MR (3)

R2: inc in each st (6)

R3: (sc 2, inc 1) *2 (8)

R4: sc in each st (8)

BIG

R1: 3 sc in MR (3)

R2: inc in each st (6)

R3: (sc 2, inc 1) *2 (8)

R4: (sc 3, inc 1) *2 (10)

R5: sc in each st (10)

Sew both the horns on the head.

Body

R1: 5 sc in MR (5)

R2: inc in each st (10)

R3: (sc 1, inc 1) * 5 (15)

R4: (sc 2, inc 1) * 5 (20)

R5: (sc 3, inc 1) * 5 (25)

R6–8: sc in each st (25)

R9: (sc 3, dec 1) * 5 (20)

R10–12: sc in each st (20)

R13: (dec 1, sc 2) * 5 (15)

FO leaving a long tail to sew.

Sew head to the body.

Ears (Make 2)

R1: 6 sc in MR (6)

R2: inc in each st (12)

FO leaving a long tail to sew. Sew ears to head.

Using pink yarn, embroider straight and stitch for nostrils.

Legs (Make 4)

Use dark grey yarn

R1: 6 sc in MR (6)

R2: sc in each st (6)

Change to body color

R3–4: sc in each st (6)

FO leaving a long tail to sew.

Sew the legs to the body.

Tail

Ch 4, sl st in 2nd ch from hook, sc, sc.

Fasten off and weave in the ends.

Sew tail to body.

Abi the Elephant

Abi the elephant is a fun wild animal that you can enjoy. Her cute little trunk makes her very inquisitive. Make her in different colors to have fun with this pattern.

What You Need:

- DK/ worsted yarn in color of your choice
- 4 mm crochet hook
- A pair of 6 mm safety eyes
- Stuffing
- Embroidery needle to sew

Head

R1: 6 sc in MR (6)

R2: sc inc in each st (12)

R3: (sc in 1 st, sc inc 1) * 6 (18)

R4:(sc in 2 sts, sc inc 1)*6 (24)

R5: (sc in 3 sts, sc inc 1) *6 (30)

R6: (sc in 4 sts, sc inc 1) *6 (36)

R7: (sc in 5 sts, sc inc 1) *6 (42)

R8–13: sc in each st (42)

Attach eyes to the head at R5

R14: (sc in 5 sts, sc dec 1) * 6 (36)

R15: (sc in 4 sts, sc dec 1) * 6 (30)

R16: (sc in 3 sts, sc dec 1) * 6 (24)

R17: (sc in 2 sts, sc dec 1) * 6 (18)

Stuff the head.

R18: (sc in 1 st, sc dec 1) * 6 (12)

R19: dec in each st (6)

Fasten off and weave in the ends.

Trunk

R1: 6 sc in MR (6)

R2: sc in each st (6)

R3: sc in 3 sts, sl st in 3 sts (6)

R4: (sc in 1 sts, sc inc 1) *3 (9)

R5–6: sc in each st (9)

R7: (sc in 2 sts, sc inc 1) *3 (12)

R8–9: sc in 2 sts, sl st in 6 sts, sc in 4 sts (12)

R10: sc in 4 sts, sl st in 4 sts, sc in 4 sts (12)

FO leaving a long tail to sew.

Sew the trunk to the front of the head.

Body

R1: 6 sc in MR (6)

R2: sc inc in each st (12)

R3: (sc in 1 st, sc inc 1) * 6 (18)

R4: (sc in 2 sts, sc inc 1) *6 (24)

R5: (sc in 3 sts, sc inc 1) *6 (30)

R6: (sc in 4 sts, sc inc 1) *6 (36)

R7–12: sc in each st (36)

R13: (sc in 4 sts, sc dec 1) * 6 (30)

R14: (sc in 3 sts, sc dec 1) * 6 (24)

R15: (sc in 2 sts, sc dec 1) * 6 (18)

Stuff the body.

R16: (sc in 1 st, sc dec 1) * 6 (12)

R17: dec in each st (6)

Fasten off and weave in the ends.

Sew the head to the body.

Arms (Make 2)

R1: 6 sc in MR (6)

R2: sc inc in each st (12)

R3–4: sc in each st (12)

R5: (sc in 4 sts, sc dec 1) *2 (10)

R6–7: sc in each st (10)

R8: (sc in 3 sts, sc dec 1) *2 (8)

R9: sc in each st (8)

Stuff lightly.

FO leaving a long tail to sew.

Attach the arms to the sides of the body.

Legs (Make 2)

R1: 6 sc in MR (6)

R2: sc inc in each st (12)

R3–8: sc in each st (12)

R9: (sc in 1 st, sc dec 1) * 4 (8)

Stuff lightly.

FO leaving a long tail to sew.

Attach the legs to the sides of the body.

Ears (Make 2)

R1: 6 sc in MR (6)

R2: sc inc in each st (12)

R3: (sc in 1 st, sc inc 1) * 6 (18)

R4: (sc in 2 sts, sc inc 1) * 6 (24)

R5–7: sc in each st (24)

R8: (sc in 6 sts, sc dec 1) *3 (21)

R9: (sc in 5 sts, sc dec 1) *3 (18)

FO leaving a long tail to sew.

Attach the ears to the head.

Tail

Ch 10 and fasten off leaving a 1 inch tail. Cut four strands of 3 inches in length and attach it along with the Ch 10 to the end of the tail. Open up the strands to make it look fluffier.

Vicky the Bear

This bear pattern is an easy one to master. With this pattern, you can go ahead and personalize it to suit various styles. So grab your hook and yarn, and create this stunning bear. Gift it to someone special or keep it for your very own collection.

What You Need:

- DK/ worsted yarn in color of your choice
- 4 mm crochet hook
- A pair of 6 mm safety eyes

- Stuffing
- Embroidery needle to sew

Head

R1: 6 sc in MR (6)

R2: sc inc in each st (12)

R3: (sc in 1 st, sc inc 1) * 6 (18)

R4: (sc in 2 sts, sc inc 1) *6 (24)

R5: (sc in 3 sts, sc inc 1) *6 (30)

R6: (sc in 4 sts, sc inc 1) *6 (36)

R7: (sc in 5 sts, sc inc 1) *6 (42)

R8–13: sc in each st (42)

Attach eyes to the head at R9

R14: (sc in 5 sts, sc dec 1) * 6 (36)

R15: (sc in 4 sts, sc dec 1) * 6 (30)

R16: (sc in 3 sts, sc dec 1) * 6 (24)

R17: (sc in 2 sts, sc dec 1) * 6 (18)

Stuff the head.

R18: (sc in 1 st, sc dec 1) * 6 (12)

R19: dec in each st (6)

Fasten off and weave in the ends.

Mouth

R1: 6 sc in MR (6)

R2: sc inc in each st (12)

R3: (sc in 1 st, sc inc 1) * 6 (18)

R4–6: sc in each st (18)

R7: (sc in 1 st, sc dec 1) * 6 (12)

Stuff the mouth.

FO leaving a long tail to sew.

Sew the mouth to the front of the head. With black yarn sew straight stitch on R2.

Body

R1: 6 sc in MR (6)

R2: sc inc in each st (12)

R3: (sc in 1 st, sc inc 1) * 6 (18)

R4: (sc in 2 sts, sc inc 1) *6 (24)

R5: (sc in 3 sts, sc inc 1) *6 (30)

R6: (sc in 4 sts, sc inc 1) *6 (36)

R7–12: sc in each st (36)

R13: (sc in 4 sts, sc dec 1) * 6 (30)

R14: (sc in 3 sts, sc dec 1) * 6 (24)

R15: (sc in 2 sts, sc dec 1) * 6 (18)

Stuff the body.

R16: (sc in 1 st, sc dec 1) * 6 (12)

R17: dec in each st (6)

Fasten off and weave in the ends.

Sew the head to the body.

Arms (Make 2)

R1: 6 sc in MR (6)

R2: sc inc in each st (12)

R3–4: sc in each st (12)

R5: (sc in 4 sts, sc dec 1) *2 (10)

R6–7: sc in each st (10)

R8: (sc in 3 sts, sc dec 1) *2 (8)

R9: sc in each st (8)

Stuff lightly.

FO leaving a long tail to sew.

Attach the arms to the sides of the body.

Legs (Make 2)

R1: 6 sc in MR (6)

R2: sc inc in each st (12)

R3–8: sc in each st (12)

R9: (sc in 1 st, sc dec 1) * 4 (8)

Stuff lightly.

FO leaving a long tail to sew.

Attach the legs to the sides of the body.

Ears (Make 2)

R1: 6 sc in MR (6)

R2: sc inc in each st (12)

R3: (sc in 1 st, sc inc 1) * 6 (18)

R4: (sc in 2 sts, sc inc 1) * 6 (24)

R5–7: sc in each st (24)

R8: (sc in 6 sts, sc dec 1)*3 (21)

R9: (sc in 5 sts, sc dec 1) *3 (18)

FO leaving a long tail to sew.

Attach the ears to the head.

Jolly the Reindeer

Have some Christmas cheer with Jolly the reindeer. Make him in festive colors to enjoy the season. You can choose to accessorize him with scarfs and bows as well. He will surely be a great addition to the family. Kids and adults love to have some cheerful holiday spirit all year round.

What You Need:

- DK/ worsted yarn in color of your choice
- White and red yarn
- 4 mm crochet hook
- A pair of 6mm safety eyes
- Stuffing
- Embroidery needle to sew

Head

R1: 6 sc in MR (6)

R2: sc inc in each st (12)

R3: (sc in 1 st, sc inc 1) * 6 (18)

R4: (sc in 2 sts, sc inc 1) *6 (24)

R5: (sc in 3 sts, sc inc 1) *6 (30)

R6: (sc in 4 sts, sc inc 1) *6 (36)

R7: (sc in 5 sts, sc inc 1) *6 (42)

R8-13: sc in each st (42)

Attach eyes to the head at R9

R14: (sc in 5 sts, sc dec 1) * 6 (36)

R15: (sc in 4 sts, sc dec 1) * 6 (30)

R16: (sc in 3sts, sc dec 1) * 6 (24)

R17: (sc in 2 sts, sc dec 1) * 6 (18)

Stuff the head.

R18: (sc in 1 st, sc dec 1) * 6 (12)

R19: dec in each st (6)

Fasten off and weave in the ends.

Mouth

With white yarn.

R1: 6 sc in MR (6)

R2: sc inc in each st (12)

R3: (sc in 1 st, sc inc 1) * 6 (18)

R4–6: sc in each st (18)

R7: (sc in 1 st, sc dec 1) * 6 (12)

Stuff the mouth.

FO leaving a long tail to sew.

Sew the mouth to the front of the head.

With red yarn, sew a nose from R1 to R3.

Body

R1: 6 sc in MR (6)

R2: sc inc in each st (12)

R3: (sc in 1 st, sc inc 1) * 6 (18)

R4: (sc in 2 sts, sc inc 1) *6 (24)

R5: (sc in 3 sts, sc inc 1) *6 (30)

R6: (sc in 4 sts, sc inc 1) *6 (36)

R7–12: sc in each st (36)

R13: (sc in 4 sts, sc dec 1) * 6 (30)

R14: (sc in 3 sts, sc dec 1) * 6 (24)

R15: (sc in 2sts, sc dec 1) * 6 (18)

Stuff the body.

R16: (sc in 1 st, sc dec 1) * 6 (12)

R17: dec in each st (6)

Fasten off and weave in the ends.

Sew the head to the body.

Legs (Make 4)

R1: 6 sc in MR (6)

R2: inc in each st (12)

R3–7: sc in each st (12)

FO leaving a long tail to sew.

Stuff the legs and sew them to the body.

Antlers (Make 2)

Long part:

R1: 6 sc in MR (6)

R2: inc in each st (12)

R3–7: sc in each st (12)

FO leaving a long tail to sew.

Short part:

R1: 6 sc in MR (6)

R2: inc in each st (12)

R3–5: sc in each st (12)

FO leaving a long tail to sew.

Now, join one short part to one long part to form a Y shape. Attach the two completed antlers to the top of the head.

Ears (Make 2)

R1: 6 sc in MR (6)

R2: inc in each st (12)

R3–4: sc in each st (12)

FO leaving a long tail to sew.

Attach the ears to the top of the head.

Scarf

Use red yarn.

Ch 30.

Hdc in each of the ch.

Fasten off and weave in the ends.

Place the scarf around the neck and secure with a knot.

Carl the Tiger

Here is a cool looking tiger that you can easily crochet. Make him a happy tiger by sewing a large smile on his face. With large buttons or safety eyes, Carl the Tiger comes to life and is ready to play with you.

What You Need:

- DK/ worsted yarn in color of your choice
- White and black yarn
- 4 mm crochet hook
- A pair of 6 mm safety eyes
- Stuffing
- Embroidery needle to sew

Head

R1: 6 sc in MR (6)

R2: sc inc in each st (12)

R3: (sc in 1 st, sc inc 1) * 6 (18)

R4: (sc in 2 sts, sc inc 1) *6 (24)

R5: (sc in 3 sts, sc inc 1) *6 (30)

R6: (sc in 4 sts, sc inc 1) *6 (36)

R7: (sc in 5 sts, sc inc 1) *6 (42)

R8: sc in each st (42)

R9: (sc in 6 sts, sc inc 1) *6 (48)

R10: sc in each st (48)

R11: (sc in 7 sts, sc inc 1) * 6 (54)

R12–17: sc in each st (54)

R18: (sc in 7 sts, sc dec 1) * 6 (48)

R19: (sc in 6 sts, sc dec 1) * 6 (42)

R20: (sc in 5 sts, sc dec 1) * 6 (36)

R21: (sc in 4 sts, sc dec 1) * 6 (30)

R22: (sc in 3 sts, sc dec 1) * 6 (24)

Stuff the head.

FO leaving a long tail to sew.

Mouth

R1: 6 sc in MR (6)

R2: sc inc in each st (12)

R3: (sc in 1 st, sc inc 1) * 6 (18)

R4: (sc in 2 sts, sc inc 1) *6 (24)

R5: (sc in 3 sts, sc inc 1) *6 (30)

FO leaving a long tail to sew.

With black yarn, sew a nose and lips to the mouth. Attach the mouth to the head. With black yarn add whiskers. Attach the safety eyes just above the mouth. Using black yarn you can add stripes by sewing straight stitches at equal intervals at the back of the head.

Body

R1: 6 sc in MR (6)

R2: sc inc in each st (12)

R3: (sc in 1 st, sc inc 1) * 6 (18)

R4: (sc in 2 sts, sc inc 1) *6 (24)

R5: (sc in 3 sts, sc inc 1) *6 (30)

R6–7: sc in each st (30)

CC black yarn

R8: sc in each st (30)

CC main color

R9-10: sc in each st (30)

CC black yarn

R11: (sc in 3 sts, sc dec 1) * 6 (24)

CC main color

R12–14: sc in each st (24)

Stuff the body.

Using the yarn left from the head sew the body and head together at the open ends.

Legs (Make 2)

R1: ch 4, sc in 2nd ch from hook, sc, 3 sc in next st, (working backwards) sc, 2 sc in last st.

R2: sc inc 1, sc, (sc inc 1) * 3, sc, (sc inc 1) * 2

R3: scinc1,sc,sc,(sc i c 1, sc)*3, sc, (sc inc 1, sc) *2

R4: sc in each st

R5: sc in 5 sts, (sc dec 1, sc in 2 sts) * 3, sc in 3 sts

R6: sc in 5 sts, (sc dec 1, sc in 1 st) * 3, sc in 3 sts

R7–8: sc in each st

FO leaving a long tail to sew.

Stuff the legs and attach to the body.

Using black yarn, you can add stripes by sewing straight stitches at equal intervals.

Arms (Make 2)

R1: 6 sc in MR (6)

R2: sc inc in each st (12)

R3–9: sc in each st (12)

FO leaving a long tail to sew.

Stuff the arms and attach to the body.

Using black yarn you can add stripes by sewing straight stitches at equal intervals.

Tail

R1: 6 sc in MR (6)

R2: (sc in 1 st, sc inc 1) * 3 (9)

R3–12: sc in each st (9)

FO leaving a long tail to sew.

Stuff the tail and attach to the body.

Ears (Make 2)

R1: 6 sc in MR (6)

R2: sc inc in each st (12)

R3: (sc in 3 sts, sc inc 1) * 3 (15)

R4–5: sc in each st (15)

FO leaving a long tail to sew.

Attach to the head.

Huan the Panda

This panda will be a great and adorable addition to your collection. With those cute looks, Huan is sure to impress everyone around. This black and white Panda is something you can easily create.

What You Need:

- DK/ worsted yarn in black and white
- 4 mm crochet hook
- A pair of 6 mm safety eyes
- Stuffing

- Embroidery needle to sew

Head

Use white yarn.

R1: 6 sc in MR (6)

R2: sc inc in each st (12)

R3: (sc in 1 st, sc inc 1) * 6 (18)

R4: (sc in 2 sts, sc inc 1) * 6 (24)

R5: (sc in 3 sts, sc inc 1) * 6 (30)

R6: (sc in 4 sts, sc inc 1) * 6 (36)

R7: (sc in 5 sts, sc inc 1) * 6 (42)

R8: sc in each st (42)

R9: (sc in 6 sts, sc inc 1) * 6 (48)

R10: sc in each st (48)

R11: (sc in 7 sts, sc inc 1) * 6 (54)

R12-17: sc in each st (54)

R18: (sc in 7 sts, sc dec 1) * 6 (48)

R19: (sc in 6 sts, sc dec 1) * 6 (42)

R20: (sc in 5 sts, sc dec 1) * 6 (36)

R21: (sc in 4 sts, sc dec 1) * 6 (30)

R22: (sc in 3 sts, sc dec 1) * 6 (24)

Stuff the head.

FO leaving a long tail to sew.

Mouth

R1: 6 sc in MR (6)

R2: sc inc in each st (12)

R3: (sc in 1 st, sc inc 1) * 6 (18)

R4: (sc in 2 sts, sc inc 1) * 6 (24)

R5–6: sc in each st (24) FO leaving a long tail to sew.

With black yarn, sew a nose and lips to the mouth. Stuff the mouth and attach the mouth to the head.

Eye Patch (Make 2)

Use black yarn

R1: Ch4, sc in 2 nd ch from hook, sc, sc inc 1, sc, sc inc 1

R2: sc inc 1, sc in 3 sts, sc inc 1, sc inc 1, sc in 3 sts, sc inc 1

R3: sc, sc inc 1, sc in 2 sts, hdc, hdc inc 1, sc in 2 sts, hdc inc 1, hdc, sc in 2 sts, sc inc 1, sc

FO leaving a long tail to sew. Attach to the head.

Attach safety eyes on the eye patch.

Body

Use white yarn.

R1: 6 sc in MR (6)

R2: sc inc in each st (12)

R3: (sc in 1 st, sc inc 1) * 6 (18)

R4: (sc in 2 sts, sc inc 1) * 6 (24)

R5: (sc in 3 sts, sc inc 1) * 6 (30)

R6–10: sc in each st (30)

R11: (sc in 3 sts, sc dec 1) * 6 (24)

CC black yarn

R12–14: sc in each st (24)

Stuff the body.

Using the yarn left over from the head sew the body and head together at the open ends.

Legs (Make 2)

R1: ch 4, sc in 2nd ch from hook, sc, 3 sc in next st, (working backwards) sc, 2 sc in last st.

R2: sc inc 1, sc, (sc inc 1) * 3, sc, (sc inc 1) * 2

R3: sc inc 1, sc, sc, (sc inc 1, sc) *3, sc, (sc inc 1, sc) *2

R4: sc in each st

R5: sc in 5 sts, (sc dec 1, sc in 2 sts) * 3, sc in 3 sts

R6: sc in 5 sts, (sc dec 1, sc in 1 st) * 3, sc in 3 sts

R7–8: sc in each st

FO leaving a long tail to sew.

Stuff the legs and attach to the body.

Arms (Make 2)

R1: 6 sc in MR (6)

R2: sc inc in each st (12)

R3–9: sc in each st (12)

FO leaving a long tail to sew.

Stuff the arms and attach to the body.

Tail

R1: 6 sc in MR (6)

R2: (sc in 1 st, sc inc 1) * 3 (9)

R3–12: sc in each st (9)

FO leaving a long tail to sew.

Stuff the tail and attach to the body.

Ears (Make 2)

R1: 6 sc in MR (6)

R2: sc inc in each st (12)

R3: (sc in 3 sts, sc inc 1) * 3 (15)

R4–5: sc in each st (15)

FO leaving a long tail to sew.

Attach to the head.

Walty the Lion

Your wild animal collection will not be complete without the king of the jungle. This lion pattern is simple and quick to make. The orange hair crocheted around the head gives it a royal look.

What You Need:

- DK/ worsted yarn in color of your choice
- Orange and white yarn
- 4 mm crochet hook
- A pair of 6 mm safety eyes
- Stuffing
- Embroidery needle to sew

Head

R1: 6 sc in MR (6)

R2: sc inc in each st (12)

R3: (sc in 1 st, sc inc 1) * 6 (18)

R4: (sc in 2 sts, sc inc 1)*6 (24)

R5: (sc in 3 sts, sc inc 1)*6 (30)

R6: (sc in 4 sts, sc inc 1)*6 (36)

R7: (sc in 5 sts, sc inc 1)*6 (42)

R8: sc in each st (42)

R9: (sc in 6 sts, sc inc 1)*6 (48)

R10: sc in each st (48)

R11: (sc in 7 sts, sc inc 1) * 6 (54)

R12–17: sc in each st (54)

R18: (sc in 7 sts, sc dec 1)*6 (48)

R19: (sc in 6 sts, sc dec 1)*6 (42)

R20: (sc in 5 sts, sc dec 1)*6 (36)

R21: (sc in 4 sts, sc dec 1) * 6 (30)

R22: (sc in 3 sts, sc dec 1) * 6 (24)

Stuff the head.

FO leaving a long tail to sew.

Mouth

Use white yarn

R1: 6 sc in MR (6)

R2: sc inc in each st (12)

R3: (sc in 1 st, sc inc 1) * 6 (18)

R4: (sc in 2 sts, sc inc 1) * 6 (24)

R5–6: sc in each st (24)

FO leaving a long tail to sew.

With orange yarn, sew a nose and with black yarn sew the lips to the mouth. Stuff the mouth and attach the mouth to the head. Attach the safety eyes just above the mouth.

Body

R1: 6 sc in MR (6)

R2: sc inc in each st (12)

R3: (sc in 1 st, sc inc 1) * 6 (18)

R4: (sc in 2 sts, sc inc 1) * 6 (24)

R5: (sc in 3 sts, sc inc 1) * 6 (30)

R6–10: sc in each st (30)

R11: (sci n 3 sts, sc dec 1)*6 (24)

R12–14: sc in each st (24)

Stuff the body.

Using the yarn left from the head sew the body and head together at the open ends.

Legs (Make 2)

R1: ch 4, sc in 2nd ch from hook, sc, 3 sc in next st, (working backwards) sc, 2 sc in last st.

R2: sc inc 1, sc, (sc inc 1) * 3, sc, (sc inc 1) * 2

R3: sc inc1 , sc, sc,(sc inc 1, sc)*3, sc, (sc inc 1, sc)*2

R4: sc in each st

R5: sc in 5 sts, (sc dec 1, sc in 2 sts) * 3, sc in 3 sts

R6: sc in 5 sts, (sc dec 1, sc in 1 st) * 3, sc in 3 sts

R7–8: sc in each st

FO leaving a long tail to sew.

Stuff the legs and attach to the body.

Arms (Make 2)

R1: 6 sc in MR (6)

R2: sc inc in each st (12)

R3–9: sc in each st (12)

FO leaving a long tail to sew.

Stuff the arms and attach to the body.

Tail

R1: Ch 15, sc in each ch.

FO leaving a long tail to sew.

Attach to the body.

Ears (Make 2)

R1: 6 sc in MR (6)

R2: sc inc in each st (12)

R3: (sc in 3 sts, sc inc 1) * 3 (15)

R4–5: sc in each st (15)

FO leaving a long tail to sew.

Attach to the head.

Using orange yarn, cut 4 5-inch strands.

Attach these to the tip of the tail using a knot.

Hair

Use orange yarn.

R1: Ch 60, turn

R2: sc in next st, (hdc in next st, {dc, tr, dc} in next st, hdc in next st, sl st in next st) * till the end.

FO leaving a long tail to sew.

Attach the hair around the head and secure it with straight stitches.

Charlie the Baby Dinosaur

This adorable baby dino pattern will leave you swooning. It is a simple pattern that you can vary in length by using larger crochet hooks. Use any color yarn you like. Add some spikes to turn the dinosaur into a different dinosaur kind. Have fun with this pattern and go wild with the variations that are possible.

What You Need:

- DK/ worsted yarn in color of your choice
- Black yarn
- 4 mm crochet hook
- A pair of 6 mm safety eyes
- Stuffing
- Embroidery needle to sew

Head

R1: 6 sc in MR (6)

R2: sc inc in each st (12)

R3–4: sc in each st (12)

R5: sc inc * 3, sc in 9 sts (15)

R6–7: sc in each st (15)

R8: sc in 6 sts, (sc in 1 st, sc dec 1) * 3 (12)

Attach safety eyes at R6

R9: (sc in 1 st, sc dec 1) * 4 (8)

Stuff the head

R10: (sc in 1 st, sc dec 1) * 2, sl st (6)

Fasten off, leaving a long tail to sew.

Neck

R1: 6 sc in MR (6)

R2–7: sc in each st (6)

Stuff the neck.

Fasten off, leaving a long tail to sew.

Attach the neck to the head.

Using black yarn, sew a mouth on the head.

Body

R1: 6 sc in MR (6)

R2: sc inc in each st (12)

R3: (sc in 1 st, sc inc 1) * 6 (18)

R4–10: sc in each st (18)

R11: (sc in 1 st, sc dec 1) * 6 (12)

Stuff the body.

R12: sc dec * 6 (6)

Fasten off leaving a long tail to sew.

Attach the body to the lower part of the neck.

Feet (Make 4)

R1: 6 sc in MR (6)

R2–7: sc in each st (6)

Stuff the neck.

Fasten off leaving a long tail to sew.

Attach the feet to the body.

Tail

R1: 4 sc in MR (4)

R2: sc in each st (4)

R3: (sc in 1 st, sc inc 1) * 2 (6)

R4: (sc in 2 sts, sc inc 1) * 2 (8)

R5: sc in each st (8)

R6: (sc in 3 sts, sc inc 1) * 2 (10)

R7: sc in each st (10)

R8: (sc in 4 sts, sc inc 1) * 2 (12)

R9: sc in each st (12)

Stuff the tail.

Fasten off, leaving a long tail to sew.

Attach the tail to the body.

Adornments (Make 3)

R1: 6 sc in MR (6)

Fasten off leaving a long tail to sew.

Attach the circles to the side of the body.

Chapter 5: The Cuties

We now introduce some of the creatures of the wild that intrigue us. We are talking about the bugs and the bees! These stunning creatures are a dream to crochet. They can be used as accessories like keychains, showpieces, etc. So crochet away these cute ones and build up your collection of the Incredibles.

Grace the Caterpillar

Isn't she a beauty? Grace the caterpillar is a colorful toy that you can easily crochet in no time. Use up any odd yarn that you have to create this beautiful toy. You can make her as long as you like by just adding additional body segments.

What You Need:

- DK/ worsted yarn in colors of your choice
- 3.5 mm crochet hook

- A pair of 6 mm safety eyes
- Stuffing
- Embroidery needle to sew

Body

R1: 6 sc in MR (6)

R2: inc in each st (12)

R3: (sc 1, inc 1) *6 (18)

R4: (sc 2, inc 1) *6 (24)

R5: (sc 3, inc 1) *6 (30)

R6: (sc 4, inc 1) *6 (36)

R7: (sc 5, inc 1) *6 (42)

R8: (sc 6, inc 1) *6 (48)

R9–16: sc in each st (48)

R17: (sc 6, dec 1) *6 (42)

R18: (sc 5, dec 1) *6 (36)

R19: (sc 4, dec 1) *6 (30)

R20: (sc 3, dec 1) *6 (24)

R21: (sc 2, dec 1) *6 (18)

First body segment made. Stuff well. Now change color to create the next segment. Stuff after each segment is created.

Repeat R4–R21 four times.

R22: (sc 1, dec 1) *6 (12)

R23: dec * 6 (6)

Stuff the body. Fasten off and weave in the ends.

Head

R1: 6 sc in MR (6)

R2: inc in each st (12)

R3: (sc 1, inc 1) *6 (18)

R4: (sc 2, inc 1) *6 (24)

R5: (sc 3, inc 1) *6 (30)

R6: (sc 4, inc 1) *6 (36)

R7: (sc 5, inc 1) *6 (42)

R8: (sc 6, inc 1) * (48)

R9: (sc 7, inc 1)*6 (54)

Attach the eyes at R4.

Sew a mouth with red yarn.

R10-17: sc in each st (54)

R18: (sc 7, dec 1) *6 (48)

R19: (sc 6, dec 1) *6 (42)

R20: (sc 5, dec 1) *6 (36)

R21: (sc 4, dec 1) *6 (30)

R22: (sc 3, dec 1) *6 (24)

R23: (sc 2, dec 1) *6 (18)

Stuff the head.

R24: (sc 1, dec 1) *6 (12)

R25: dec * 6 (6)

Fasten off and weave in the ends. Sew the head to the body.

Antennae (Make 2)

R1: 6 sc in MR (6)

R2: inc in each st (12)

R3: (sc 3, inc 1) * 3 (15)

R4–6: sc in each st (15)

R7: (sc 1, dec 1) * 6 (10)

R8–12: sc in each st (10)

FO leaving a long tail to sew. Sew the antennae on the head.

Feet (Make 10)

Ch 8, hdc in 3 nd ch from hook, hdc in remaining ch.

FO leaving a long tail to sew.

Sew two feet onto each of the body segments.

Oscar the Owl

Here is an all-time favorite toy that kids and adults adore. We give you a tiny pattern that can be used for various things like ornaments, keychains, etc. So have fun with this pattern and choose bright and bold colors to give your owl the edge.

What You Need:

- DK/ worsted yarn in color of your choice
- White and pink yarn
- 3 mm crochet hook
- A pair of black buttons
- Stuffing

- Embroidery needle to sew

Body

Use yarn color of your choice (A)

R1: 6 sc in MR (6)

R2: inc in each st (12)

R3: (sc 1, inc 1) *6 (18)

R4: (sc 2, inc 1) *6 (24)

R5: (sc 3, inc 1) *6 (30)

R6: (sc 4, inc 1) *6 (36)

R7: (sc 5, inc 1) *6 (42)

R8: (sc 6, inc 1) *6 (48)

R9: (sc 7, inc 1) *6 (54)

R10–20: sc in each st (54)

R21: (sc 7, dec 1) *6 (48)

R22: sc in each st (48)

R23: (sc 6, dec 1) *6 (42)

R24: sc in each st (42)

R25: (sc 5, dec 1) *6 (36)

R26: sc in each st (36)

R27: (sc 4, dec 1) * 6 (30)

R28: sc in each st (30)

Stuff the body well.

Fold the body and sc across the top to close the gap.

Eyes (Make 2)

Use white yarn

R1: 6sc in MR (6)

R2: inc in each st (12)

R3: (sc 1, inc 1) * 6 (18)

FO leaving a long tail to sew.

Place the eyes on the body keeping a distance of 3 sts in between.

Place a black button in the center of each eye and sew the eyes in place.

Beak

Use pink yarn

Ch4, sl st in 2 nd ch from hook, sc in the next 2 sts.

FO leaving a long tail to sew.

Sew the beak in place.

Ginnie the Ladybug

This ladybug is a bright and eye-catching toy that you can crochet with ease. Ginnie is used as a pincushion here. You can choose to play with her or use her as a keychain too. So the ideas are endless. Make many and give them as a gift to your loved ones too.

What You Need:

- DK/ worsted yarn in red and black
- 4 mm crochet hook
- A pair of 3 mm safety eyes
- Wire antennae
- Stuffing
- Embroidery needle to sew

Body

TOP HALF

Use red yarn

R1: 6 sc in MR (6)

R2: sc inc in each st (12)

R3: (sc in 1 st, sc inc 1) * 6 (18)

R4: (sc in 2 sts, sc inc 1) *6 (24)

R5: (sc in 3sts, sc inc 1) *6 (30)

R6: (sc in 4 sts, sc inc 1) *6 (36)

R7: (sc in 5 sts, sc inc 1) *6 (42)

R8–16: sc in each st (42)

Fasten off.

BOTTOM HALF

Use black yarn.

R1: 6 sc in MR (6)

R2: sc inc in each st (12)

R3: (sc in 1 st, sc inc 1) * 6 (18)

R4: (sc in 2 sts, sc inc 1) * 6 (24)

R5: (sc in 3 sts, sc inc 1) * 6 (30)

R6: (sc in 4 sts, sc inc 1) * 6 (36)

R7: (sc in 5 sts, sc inc 1) * 6 (42)

R8: sc in each st (42)

Fasten off.

Sew the top and bottom half of the body together. Stuff as you go.

Head

Use black yarn

R1: 6 sc in MR (6)

R2: sc inc in each st (12)

R3: (sc in 1 st, sc inc 1) * 6 (18)

R4: (sc in 2 sts, sc inc 1) * 6 (24)

R5-8: sc in each st (24)

R9: (sc in 2 sts, sc dec 1) *6 (18)

Stuff the head.

Fasten off, leaving a long tail to sew.

Attach the head to the body.

Using red yarn sew a mouth to the head.

Using black yarn sew a straight stitch in the center of the body.

Attach the wire antennae to the head.

Legs (Make 6)

Use black yarn

R1: 4 sc in MR (4)

R2–4: sc in each st (4)

Fasten off leaving a long tail to sew.

Attach the legs to the body.

Dots (Make 6)

Use black yarn

R1: 6 sc in MR (6)

R2: sc inc in each st (12)

Fasten off leaving a long tail to sew.

Attach the dots around the body and sew in place.

Trisha the Bee

Another buzzing companion you can crochet is Trisha the Bee. She is waiting to zoom around in your garden. So crochet this quick pattern and have fun. You can easily create many little bees in a short span of time. So enjoy filling your garden with these cuties, or best yet, gift them to friends.

What You Need:

- DK/ worsted yarn in yellow and black
- White, black, and yellow yarn
- 2 mm crochet hook
- A pair of 3 mm safety eyes
- Stuffing
- Embroidery needle to sew

Body

Use yellow yarn

R1: 6 sc in MR (6)

R2: sc inc in each st (12)

R3: (sc in 1 st, sc inc 1) * 6 (18)

R4: (sc in 2 sts, sc inc 1) *6 (24)

R5: (sc in 3 sts, sc inc 1) *6 (30)

R6: (sc in 4 sts, sc inc 1) *6 (36)

R7: (sc in 5 sts, sc inc 1) *6 (42)

R8–10: sc in each st (42)

CC black yarn

R11--13: sc in each st (42)

CC yellow yarn

R14–17: sc in each st (42)

CC black yarn

R18–20: sc in each st (42)

CC yellow yarn

R21–22: sc in each st (42)

R23: (sc in 5 sts, sc dec 1) *6 (36)

R24: (sc in 4 sts, sc dec 1) *6 (30)

R25:(sc in 3 sts, sc dec 1) *6 (24)

R26: (sc in 2 sts, sc dec 1) *6 (18)

Stuff the body.

R27: (sc in 1 st, sc dec 1) *6 (12)

R28: dec in each st (6)

Fasten off and weave in the ends.

Attach safety eyes to the front of the body.

Antennae (Make 2)

Using black yarn, Ch 6 and fasten off.

Attach this to the top of the head.

Tail

Use black yarn.

R1: 4 sc in MR (4)

R2–7: sc in each st (4)

R8: (sc in 1 st, sc inc) *2 (6)

Fasten off leaving a long tail to sew.

Attach the tail to the body.

Legs (Make 6)

Use black yarn

R1: 4 sc in MR (4)

R2-4: sc in each st (4)

Fasten off leaving a long tail to sew.

Attach the legs to the body.

Wings (Make 2)

Use white yarn

R1: 6 sc in MR (6)

R2: sc inc in each st (12)

R3: (sc in 1 st, sc inc 1) * 6 (18)

R4: sl st in 9 sts, (sc in 2 sts, sc inc 1) *3 (21)

Fasten off leaving a long tail to sew.

Attach the wings to the top of the body.

Bernie the Bat

Bernie the Bat may look scary but she is a doll to have around. This is a pretty simple pattern to work with. Create the bat in various colors for a whole range of toys. Change the crochet hook size to have the same pattern in different sizes.

What You Need:

- DK/ worsted yarn in color of your choice
- White and black yarn
- White felt
- 3 mm crochet hook
- A pair of 8 mm safety eyes
- Stuffing
- Embroidery needle to sew

Body

Use yarn color of your choice

R1: 6 sc in MR (6)

R2: sc inc in each st (12)

R3: (sc in 1 st, sc inc 1) * 6 (18)

R4: (sc in 2 sts, sc inc 1) * 6 (24)

R5: (sc in 3 sts, sc inc 1) * 6 (30)

R6: (sc in 4 sts, sc inc 1) * 6 (36)

R7: (sc in 5 sts, sc inc 1) * 6 (42)

R8–13: sc in each st (42)

R14: (sc in 5 sts, sc dec 1)*6 (36)

R15: (sc in 4 sts, sc dec 1)*6 (30)

You can now attach the eyes between R12 and R13 with 6 sts in between. Using black yarn, sew a mouth on R14.

R16: (sc in 3 sts, sc dec 1) *6 (24)

R17: (sc in 2 sts, sc dec 1) *6 (18)

Stuff the body.

R18: (sc in 1 st, sc dec 1) *6 (12)

R19: dec in each st (6)

Fasten off and weave in the ends.

Ears (Make 2)

R1: 5 sc in MR (5)

R2: sc inc 1, (sc in 2 sts, sc inc 1) * 2 (8)

R3: (sc in 1 st, sc inc 1) * 4 (12)

R4: (sc in 2 sts, sc inc 1) * 4 (16)

R5: (sc in 3 sts, sc inc 1) * 4 (20)

R6:(sc in 3 sts, sc dec 1)*4 (16)

R7: (sc in 2 sts, sc dec 1)*4 (12)

Fasten off, leaving a long tail to sew.

Sew the ears to the top of the body.

Wings (Make 2)

R1: Ch12, turn

R2: (sl st, sc in 4 sts, sc dec, sl st) * 4, ch1, turn

R3: sc inc, sc inc, sc in 8 sts, ch1, turn

R4: sc in 3 sts, sc dec, sc in 5 sts, ch1, turn

R5: sc in 3 sts, sc dec, sc in 4 sts, ch1, turn

R6: sl st in 5 sts, ch2, sl st

Fasten off, leaving a long tail to sew.

Attach the wings between R10 and R14.

You can cut out tiny teeth from the white felt and glue it onto the mouth.

Chapter 6: Big Size Animals

Mr. Big Bunny

Mr. Big Bunny is 22 inches in length. You may choose to make it using a single color or multi-colored like Mr. Big Bunny here. Bunnies are one of the trendiest animals to crochet for amigurumi crocheters. The cute face, the long ears and the softail make anyone fall in love with them!

What You Need:

- 6 mm crochet hook
- cotton flannel fabric in a color of your choice
- two 15 mm safety eyes
- large pompom maker (9 cm diameter)
- colored tapestry wool (color of your choice)
- red ribbon for the bowtie
- stuffing
- stitch markers
- sewing thread
- sewing needle
- tapestry needle

Head

R1: 6 sc in MR (6)

R2: inc *6 (12)

R3: (inc, sc in next st) *6 (18)

R4: (inc, sc in next 2 st) *6 (24)

R5: (inc, sc in next 3 st) *6 (30)

R6: (inc, sc in next 4 st) *6 (36)

R7: (inc, sc in next 5 st) *6 (42)

R8: (inc, sc in next 6 st) *6 (48)

R9: (inc, sc in next 7 st) *6 (54)

R10: (inc, sc in next 8 st) *6 (60)

R11 – 18 (8 rounds): sc in each st around (60)

R19: (dec, sc in next 8 st) *6 (54)

R20: (dec, sc in next 7 st) *6 (48)

R21: (dec, sc in next 6 st) *6 (42)

Insert the safety eyes between rounds 16 and 17 approx. 16 st apart.

Start stuffing the head and continue as you go.

R22: (dec, sc in next 5 st) *6 (36)

R23: (dec, sc in next 4 st) *6 (30)

R24: (dec, sc in next 3 st) *6 (24)

Fasten off and weave in the ends.

Use pink thread to sew the nose between rounds 15 and 17 making long stitches to create a pink triangle.

Use black thread to sew the mouth under the nose between rounds 18 and 20.

Ears (Make 2)

R1: start 6 sc in MR (6)

R2: (inc, sc in next 2 st) *2 (8)

R3: (inc, sc in next 3 st) *2 (10)

R4: (inc, sc in next 4 st) *2 (12)

R5: (inc, sc in next 5 st) *2 [14]

R6: (inc, sc in next 6 st) *2 [16]

R7–21 (15 rounds): sc in each st around (16)

R22: dec, sc in next 14 st (15)

R23: sc in each st around (15)

R24: dec, sc in next 13 st (14)

R25: sc in each st around (14)

R26: dec, sc in next 12 st (13)

R27: sc in each st around (13)

R28: dec, sc in next 11 st (12)

R29: sc in each st around (12)

R30: dec, sc in next 10 st (11)

R31: sc in each st around (11)

R32: dec, sc in next 9 st (10)

R33: sc in each st around (10)

Do not stuff.

Fasten off leaving a long tail for sewing the ears between rounds 6 and 8 of the head.

Body

R1: start 6 sc in MR (6)

R2: inc *6 (12)

R3: (inc, sc in next st) *6 (18)

R4: (inc, sc in next 2 st) *6 (24)

R5: (inc, sc in next 3 st) *6 (30)

R6: (inc, sc in next 4 st) *6 (36)

R7: (inc, sc in next 5 st) *6 (42)

R8: (inc, sc in next 6 st) *6 (48)

R9–13: sc in each st around (48)

R14: (dec, sc in next 6 st) *6 (42)

R15–17: sc in each st around (42)

R18: (dec, sc in next 5 st) *6 (36)

R19–21: sc in each st around (36)

R22: (dec, sc in next 4 st) *6 (30)

R23–25: sc in each st around (30)

R26: (dec, sc in next 3 st) *6 (24)

Stuff the body.

Fasten off leaving a long tail for sewing the body to the head.

Arms (Make 2)

R1: start 6 sc in MR (6)

R2: inc *6 (12)

R3–9: sc in each st around (12)

R10: dec, sc in next 10 st (11)

R11–12: sc in each st around (11)

R13: dec, sc in next 9 st (10)

R14–19: sc in each st around (10)

Stuff lightly.

Fasten off. Leave a long tail to sew the arms to the body.

Legs (Make 2)

R1: start 6 sc in MR (6)

R2: inc *6 (12)

R3: (inc, sc in next st) *6 (18)

R4: (inc, sc in next 2 st) *6 (24)

R5–9: sc in each st around (24)

R10: (dec, sc in next 6 st) *3 (21)

R11: sc in each st around (21)

R12: (dec, sc in next 5 st) *3 (18)

R13–15: sc in each st around (18)

R16: (dec, sc in next 4 st) *3 (15)

R17–19: sc in each st around (15)

R20: (dec, sc in next 3 st) *3 times (12)

R21–23: sc in each st around (12)

R24: (dec, sc in next 2 st) *3 times (9)

R25–27: sc in each st around (9)

Stuff lightly.

Fasten off. Leave a long tail to sew the legs to the body.

Tail

Make a 3.5 inches' diameter pompom using a pompom maker.

Cut a long tail of yarn to thread the pompom around the center. Use the same tail to sew the pompom to the back of the body.

To add a bowtie, simply create it using the red ribbon or any other color of your choice.

Mr. Gary the Giraffe

How cute is Mr. Gary?! This is a pretty simple pattern to work with. You will use various colors and switch as you stitch. Change the crochet hook size to have the same pattern in different sizes.

What You Need:

- DK/ worsted yarn in colors (Orange, blue, pink, tan, green, light pink, brown, and purple)
- A pair of 6 mm safety eyes
- Stuffing
- 3 mm hook
- Embroidery needle to sew

Head

Use white

R1: Ch 2, 6 sc in second ch from hook

R2: sc 2 in each sc around (12)

R3: (sc 1, 2 sc in next sc) *6 (18)

R4: (sc 2, 2 sc in next sc) *6 (24)

R5: (sc 3, 2 sc in next sc) *6 (30)

R6: (sc 4, 2 sc in next sc) *6 (36)

R7–10: sc 36

Switch color to purple.

R11–12: sc 36

Switch color to yellow.

R13: sc 36

R14: (sc 5, 2 sc in next sc) *6 (42)

Switch color to red.

R15: (sc 6, 2 sc in next sc) *6 (48)

R16: sc (48)

Switch color to green.

R17–18: sc (48)

Switch color to light pink.

R19: (sc 6, dec 1) *6 (42)

R20: (sc 4, dec 1) *7 (35)

Sew on face.

Switch color to blue.

R21: (sc 3, dec 1) *7 (28)

R22: (sc 2, dec 1) *7 (21)

Stuff firmly. Switch color to pink.

R23: (sc 1, dec 1) * 7 (14)

R24: dec 1 *7 (7)

Fasten off and weave in the ends.

Ears (Make 2)

Use orange.

R1: Ch 2, 6 sc in second ch from hook

R2: sc 2 in each sc around (12)

R3: (sc 1, 2 sc in next sc) *6 (18)

R4–9: Sc 18

Fasten off. leave a long tail to sew together.

Horns (Make 2)

Use white

R1: Ch 2, 6 sc in second ch from hook

R2: sc 2 in each sc around (12)

R3–R5: sc 12

R6: dec 1 *6 (6)

R7–R13: sc 6

Fasten off. Leave a long tail to sew together. Stuff firmly.

Arms (Make 2)

Use white.

R1: Ch 2, 6 sc in second ch from hook

R2: sc 2 in each sc around (12)

R3: (sc 1, 2 sc in next sc) *6 (18)

R4–5: sc 18

R6: sc 1, dec 1 (12)

Change color

R7–R23: sc 12

Fasten off. Leave a long tail to sew together. Stuff tightly.

Switch colors every two rows.

Legs (Make 2)

Use white.

R1: Ch 2, 6 sc in second ch from hook

R2: sc 2 in each sc around (12)

R3: (sc 1, 2 sc in next sc) *6 (18)

R4: (sc 2, 2 sc in next sc) *6 (24)

R5–R8: sc 24

R9: (sc 2, dec) *6 (18)

R10: (sc 1, dec) *6 times (12)

Switch color.

Switch colors every two rows.

R11–R33: sc 12

Fasten off. Leave a long tail to sew together.

Stuff firmly.

Body

Use red.

R1: Ch 2, 6 sc in second ch from hook

R2: sc 2 in each sc around (12)

R3: (sc 1, 2 sc in next sc) *6 (18)

R4: (sc 2, 2 sc in next sc) *6 (24)

R5: (sc 3, 2 sc in next sc) *6 (30)

R6: (sc 4, 2 sc in next sc) *6 (36)

Switch color to purple.

R7: (sc 5, 2 sc in next sc) *6 (42)

R8: (sc 6, 2 sc in next sc) *6 (48)

Switch color to orange.

R9: (sc 7, 2 sc in next sc) *6 (54)

R10: sc (54)

Switch color to light green.

R11–12: sc (54)

Switch color to white.

R13–14: sc (54)

Switch color to pink.

R15–16: sc (54)

Switch color to blue.

R17–18: sc (54)

Switch color to yellow.

R19: Sc54

R20: (sc 7, dec 1) *6 (48)

Switch color to green.

R21: (sc 6, dec 1) *6 (42)

R22: (sc 5, dec 1) *6 (36)

Switch color to tan.

R23: (sc 4, dec 1) *6 (30)

Stuff firmly

R24: (sc 3, dec 1) *6 (24)

Switch color to pink.

R25–26: sc (24)

Switch color to red.

R27–28: sc (24)

Switch color to white.

R29–30: sc (24)

Switch color to brown.

R31–32: sc (24)

Switch color to light green.

R33–34: sc (24)

Switch color to pink.

R35–36: sc (24)

Stuff firmly.

Fasten off and weave in the ends.

Mr. Rob the Rooster

Isn't Mr. Rob so funny and adorable? This may look like a complicated pattern, but if you closely follow the instructions, you will do a great job in creating this special character. You may also crochet another rooster, and give it a name yourself!

What You Need:

- DK/ worsted yarn in colors (yellow, orange, red, brown, and white)
- 1.5 mm hook
- Stuffing
- Metal wire with a diameter of 0.9–1.0 mm
- Adhesive tape
- A pair or 10 mm safety eyes,
- A pair of artificial eye lashes

Head

Use orange.

R1: 6 sc in MR

R2: 6 inc (12)

R3: (1 sc, inc) *6 (18)

R4:: (2 sc, inc) *6 (24)

R5: (3 sc, inc) *6 (30)

R6: (4 sc, inc) *6 (36)

R7–12: 36 sc

R13: 6 sc, 6 inc, 12 sc, 6 inc, 6 sc (48)

R14: 6 sc, (1 sc, inc) *6, 12 sc, (inc, 1 sc) *6 , 6 sc (60)

R15–20: 60 sc

R21: 60 sc,1 sc to move the beginning.

R22: 6 sc, (1 sc, dec) *6 , 12 sc, (dec, 1sc) *6 , 6 sc (48)

R23: 6 sc, 6 dec, 12 sc, 6 dec, 6 sc (36)

R24: (4 sc, dec) *6 times (30)

R25: (3 sc, dec) *6 times (24)

R26: (2 sc, dec) *6 times (18)

R27: 18 sc

Stuff well.

Fasten off and weave in the ends.

Beak

(Upper)

Use yellow.

R1: 3 sc in MR

R2: 3 inc (6)

R3: (1 sc, inc) *3 (9)

R4: 9 sc

R5: (2 sc, inc)*3 (12)

R6: 12 sc

R7: (3 sc, inc)*3 (15)

R8: (4 sc, inc) *3 (18)

R9: (2 sc, inc) *6 (24)

R10: (3 sc, inc) *6 (30)

R11: (4 sc, inc) *6 (36)

R12: (5 sc, inc) *6 (42)

R13: (6 sc, inc) *6 (48)

R14–16: 48 sc,

Finish and cut off the yarn.

(Lower)

Use yellow.

R1: 3 sc in MR

R2: 3 inc *6)

R3: (1 sc, inc) *3 (9)

R4: 9 sc

R5: (2 sc, inc) *3 (12)

R6: 12 sc

R7: (3 sc, inc) *3 (15)

R8: (4 sc, inc) *3 (18)

R9: (2 sc, inc) *6 (24)

R10: (3 sc, inc) *6 (30)

R11: (4 sc, inc) *6 (36)

R12: (5 sc, inc) *6 (42)

R13: (6 sc, inc) *6 (48)

R14-16: 48 sc.

Finish, cut off the yarn.

Legs

Use brown.

Big toe (Make 2)

R1: 6 sc in MR

R2: 6 inc (12)

R3–4: 12 sc

R5: (1 sc, dec) *4 (8)

R6: (2 sc, dec) * 2 (6)

R7–12: 6 sc

Finish by cutting off the yarn and stuffing the toes.

Toe (Make 2)

R1: 6 sc in MR

R2: 6 inc (12)

R3–4: 12 sc

R5: (1 sc, dec) *4 (8)

R6: (2 sc, dec) *2 (6)

R7–11: 6 sc

For the last toe: Don't cut the yarn, stuff the toe. Collect the toes in a foot.

Foot

R1: 3 sc along the 1st toe, 3 sc along the big toe, 6 sc along the 2nd toe, 3 sc along the big toe, 3 sc along the 1st toe 18 sc

R2–3: 18 sc

R4: (1 sc, dec) *6 (12)

R5: 2 sc, 3 ch, skip 3 sc, 7 sc (12)

R6: 2 sc, 3 sc in chains, 7 sc (12)

R7 rnd: 6 dec (6)

R8–9: 6 sc

R10: (1 sc, inc) *3 (9)

R11: 9 sc

R12: (1 sc , dec) *3 (6)

Finish by cutting off the yarn and closing the hole using a needle.

Leg

8 sc around the hole in the center of the foot.

R1–7: 8 sc

R8: (2 sc, dec) *2 (6)

R9–14: 6 sc.

Use orange.

R15: 6 inc (12)

R16: 12 sc

R17: (1 sc, inc) *6 (18)

R18–19: 18 sc

R20: (2 sc, inc) *6 (24)

R21: 24 sc

Fasten off and leave a long tail to sew other parts.

Wings

Use orange.

The first feather (Make 2)

R1: 6 sc in MR

R2: 6 inc (12)

R3–5: 12 sc

R6: (1 sc, dec) *4 (8)

R7–10: 8 sc

The second feather (Make 2)

R1: 6 sc in MR

R2: 6 inc (12)

R3–5: 12 sc

R6: (1 sc, dec) *4 (8)

R7–12: 8 sc

The third feather (Make 2)

R1: 6 sc in MR

R2: 6 inc (12)

R3–5: 12 sc

R6 rnd (1 sc, dec) *4 (8)

R7–14: 8 sc

The fourth feather (Make 2)

R1: 6 sc in MR

R2: 6 inc (12)

R3–5: 12 sc

R6: (1 sc, dec) *4 (8)

R7–16: 8 sc

Keep the yarn and don't stop the feathers.

Attach feathers without replacing your row marker.

R17: 4 sc along the fourth feather, 8 sc along the third, 4 along the fourth, 16 sc

R18: 16 sc

R19: 8 sc, apply the second feather, make 8 sc along the second feather, 8 sc (24)

R20: 24 sc

R21: 12 sc, 8 sc along the first feather, 12 sc (32)

R22: 32 sc

R23: 8 sc, dec, 12 sc, dec, 8 sc (30)

R24: 7 sc, dec, 12 sc, dec, 7 sc (28)

R25: 6 sc, dec, 12 sc, dec, 6 sc (26)

R26: 5 sc, dec, 12 sc, dec, 5 sc (24)

R27: 4 sc, dec, 12 sc, dec, 4 sc (22)

R28: 3 sc, dec, 12 sc, dec, 3 sc (20)

R29: 2 sc, dec, 12 sc, dec, 2 sc (18)

R30: 1 sc, dec, 12 sc, dec, 1 sc (16)

R31: dec, 12, dec (14)

R32: dec, 10, dec (12)

R33–36: 12 sc

Finish. Leave a long tale to sew other parts.

Install a wire in the longest feather.

Body

R1: 6 sc

R2: 6 inc (12)

R3: (1 sc, inc) *6 (18)

R4: (2 sc, inc) *6 (24)

R5: (3 sc, inc) *6 (30)

R6: (4 sc, inc) * 6 (36)

R7: (5 sc, inc) *6 (42)

R8: (6 sc, inc) *6 (48)

R9: (7 sc, inc) *6 (54)

R10: 1 ch, skip 1 st, 7 sc, inc, 8 sc, inc, 3 sc, 1 ch, skip 1 st, 4 sc, inc, (8 sc, inc) *3 (60)

R11: (9 sc, inc) *6 (66)

Make 1sc in the chains of the previous round.

R12: (10 sc, inc) *6 (72)

R13: (11 sc, inc) *6 (78)

R14-22: 78 sc

R23: 3 sc, (2 sc, dec) * 6, 51 sc (72)

R24: 3 sc, (1 sc, dec) *6, 51 sc (66)—this is where tail goes.

R25–27: 66 sc.

Install the leg wireframes, twist and separate.

R28: (9 sc, dec) *6 (60)

R29: (8 sc, dec) *6 (54)

R30: (7 sc, dec) * 6 (48)

R31: (6 sc, dec) *6 (42)

R32: (5 sc, dec) * 6 (36)

R33: (4 sc, dec) *6 (30)

Install the wing frames at the R27. Attach to the spine.

R34: (3 sc, dec) *6 (24)

R35: 24 sc

R36: (2 sc, dec) *6 (18)

R37-39: 18 sc

R40: (1 sc, dec) *6 (12)

R41–51: 12 sc

R52: (1 sc, inc) *6 (18)

Sew the wings.

Install the spine frame in the head.

Sew the head.

Sew the legs to the body.

Tail feathers (Make 3)

R1: 6 sc in MR

R2: 6 inc (12)

R3: (2 sc, inc) *4 (16)

R4–6: 16 sc

R7: (2 sc, dec) *4 (12)

R8-10: 12 sc

R11: (dec, 4 sc) *2 (10)

R12–14: 10 sc

R15: (dec, 3 sc) *2 (8)

R16-18: 8 sc

R19: (dec, 2 sc) * 2 (6)

R20–22: 6 sc

Connect all feathers using orange yarn.

R1: 3 sc along the first feather, 3 sc along the second, 6 sc along the third, 3 sc along the second, 3 sc along the first, 18 sc

R2: 18 sc

R3: (1 sc, dec) *6 (12)

R4: (1 sc, inc) *6 (18)

R5: (2 sc, inc) * 6 (24)

R6: 24 sc

Finish and leave a long tail.

Cockscomb

First part

R1: 6 sc in MR

R2: 6 inc (12)

R3: (1 sc, inc) *6 (18)

R4–6: 18 sc

R7: (1 sc, dec) *6 (12)

R8–10: 12 sc

R11: (dec, 4 sc) * 2 (10)

R12–15: 10 sc

R16: (dec, 3 sc) * 2 (8)

R17–19: 8 sc

Second part

R1: 6 sc in MR

R2: 6 inc (12)

R3: (1 sc, inc) *6 (18)

R4–6: 18 sc

R7: (1 sc , dec) * 6 (12)

R8–10: 12 sc

R11: (dec, 4 sc) * 2 (10)

R12–15: 10 sc

R16: (dec, 3 sc) *2 (8)

R17: 8 sc

Third part

R1: 6 sc in MR

R2: 6 inc (12)

R3: (2 sc, inc) * 4 (16)

R4–6: 16 sc

R7: (2 sc, dec) *4 (12)

R8–9: 12 sc

R10: (dec, 4 sc) * 2 (10)

R11–13: 10 sc

R14: (dec, 3 sc) * 2 (8)

Connect all parts.

R15: 4 sc for the small part, 4 sc for the middle part, 8 sc for the big part, 4 sc for the middle part, 4 sc for the small part (24)

R16: 24 sc

Attach to the head.

Beard (Make 2)

R1: 6 sc in MR

R2: 6 inc (12)

R3: (1 sc, inc) *6 (18)

R4–5: 18 sc

R6: (1 sc, dec) *6 (12)

R7–9: 12 sc

R10: 6 dec (6)

R11–12: 6 sc

Connect both beads using 3 sc.

Join the beak.

Eyes (Make 2)

Use white.

R1: 6 sc in MR (6)

R2: inc *6 (12)

R3: (1sc, inc) *6 (18)

R4: 18 sc (18)

R5: (1sc, dec) *6 (12)

Stuff lightly.

Install the eyes between the R2–3.

R6: dec *6 (6)

Join to the head.

Add eyelashes.

Conclusion

The Therapeutic Benefits of Crocheting

Crocheting—or any other form of yarn crafts is a fun way to entertain yourself, especially when you are knitting something for a loved one. However, there are other great benefits of knitting, such as using it as a way to relieve anxiety and depression. It has been scientifically proven that knitting patterns releases serotonin, which is a natural antidepressant, in the brain. In 2015, CNN reported that "in one study of more than 3,500 knitters, published in *The British Journal of Occupational Therapy*, 81% of [the] respondents with depression reported feeling happy after knitting. More than half reported feeling "very happy."" (CNN).

Stress is one of the leading causes to our health problems. Stress may be the cause of migraines, tiredness, memory loss, and even heart failure. It is well known that by reducing stress, we tend to decrease our chances of suffering from various diseases. Spending time daily on knitting or crocheting as meditation will surely diminish the effects of stress in our lives.

Any form of knitting keeps your hands busy and your mind focused, which in turn reduced excessive thinking and anxiety. It actually transfers the mind to a serene space, and that is due to the repetitive nature of the work; for example, stitching designs and counting stitches. Knitting and crocheting have also been proven to be very helpful for those who suffer from Obsessive Compulsive Disorders as well as those who suffer from eating disorders.

According to the American Counselling Association, one study showed that nearly ¾ of women with anorexia found knitting to be calming and anxiety-reducing. (Polino).

In addition, working on a yarn project makes a person feel productive and, hence, builds self-esteem. When you knit, you tend to learn new skills, feel ambitious as you busy yourself in useful means to give to others, and express yourself in a beautiful way. By simply using your imagination, and then focusing on and creating a handcraft will definitely boost your confidence.

The art of crochet amigurumi is especially beneficial for the elderly for it has been proven to reduce dementia that is related to growing in age. Yonas Geda, MD, a neuropsychiatrist and researcher at the Mayo Clinic, finalized a study which revealed that knitting is neuroprotective and can lessen dementia by as much as 50%. (Polino)

Even if you suffer from insomnia, you will find that knitting and doing yarn crafts can rescue you from disrupted sleep patterns. As you concentrate on a soft, simple, repetitively patterned crochet or knit project, you will find that both your body and mind are pacified. Herbert Benson of the Mind/Body Medical Institute, conducted a study which showed that all insomnia patients testified that their sleep has improved with 90% being able to let go of medication while being in a program that consisted of . . . knitting (Caiola).

Exclusive 5-day bonus course just for you!

We will be sharing top crafting mistakes to avoid, how to save money on supplies and extra craft patterns!

Simply let us know where to send the course e-mails to via this link below.

https://bit.ly/nancy-gordon

For any general feedback & enquiries, you can reach us at bookgrowthpublishing@mail.com

References

Alison. *Crochet Giraffe.* 15 Nov. 2015, www.flickr.com/photos/kornflakestew/22389466923. Accessed 8 Jan. 2021.

Caiola, Sammy. "The health benefits of knitting." Chicagotribune.com, 7 Oct. 2014, www.chicagotribune.com/lifestyles/health/sns-mct-bc-health-knitting-20141007-story.html. Accessed 5 Jan. 2021.

Celiberto, Francesca. (2012, September 29). *Crochet whale.* Flickr. https://www.flickr.com/photos/154962637@N06/39112578920

Clio1789. "Tiny Turtle." *Flickr*, 22 Apr. 2008, www.flickr.com/photos/clio1789/2512946270.

CNN, Jacque Wilson. "This is your brain on crafting." *CNN*, 5 Jan. 2015, www.edition.cnn.com/2014/03/25/health/brain-crafting-benefits/index.html. Accessed 5 Jan. 2021.

Dallaway, J. (2015, January 1). *Crocheted pig.* Flickr. https://www.flickr.com/photos/janed/15978241740

Danilyuk, Pavel. *Woman in Brown Coat and Knit Cap*, www.pexels.com/photo/cold-wood-people-woman-5788315/.

Emma. *Crochet Lenny Rabbit.* 2 Feb. 2013, www.flickr.com/photos/lululoves1000. Accessed 7 Jan. 2020.

Ginrei. "Boney the Crochet Dog." *Flickr*, 7 Feb. 2008, www.flickr.com/photos/42869864@N00/3210613071. Accessed 4 Jan. 2021.

Gordon, Mona. *Crochet Rooster*, 1 Jan. 2018, www.flickr.com/photos/158058729@N02/30173135157. Accessed 8 Jan. 2021.

gray la gran. "Swap 020." *Flickr*, 19 Jan. 2012, www.flickr.com/photos/54706746@N00/6762732805. Accessed 4 Jan. 2021.

Hoerwin56. *Easter Bunny Crochet Fabric*, www.pixabay.com/photos/easter-bunny-crochet-fabric-figure-1286796/.

Hole, Tiny. "Pusheen from Messenger Amigurumi." *Flickr*, 30 Oct. 2017, www.flickr.com/photos/153257483@N06/26622794638. Accessed 7 Jan. 2021.

Hunt, Ericka. "Batty Betty." *Flickr*, 19 Oct. 2009, www.flickr.com/photos/erickacrafts/4036132424. Accessed 7 Jan. 2021.

K, Elsa. "Felt Pincushions08." *Flickr*, 10 June 2015, www.flickr.com/photos/blueraindrops-crafts/42232247154. Accessed 7 Jan. 2021.

Lauren. "Heffa 2." *Flickr*, 18 Feb. 2009, www.flickr.com/photos/lt81/3434644668. Accessed 7 Jan. 2021.

Ligitos. "Necklace Crab." *Flickr*, 12 Mar. 2008, www.flickr.com/photos/ligitos/2366455754. Accessed 4 Jan. 2021.

Lille, Designs by Mari-Liis. "Little Duck." *Flickr*, 12 Feb. 2017, www.flickr.com/photos/lilleliis/23653777458. Accessed 7 Jan. 2021.

MagicalAmigurumi. "Beige Alpaca." *Flickr*, 31 Mar. 2012, www.flickr.com/photos/63325837@N06/6887607188. Accessed 7 Jan. 2021.

Marije. "Sheep." *Flickr*, 15 Mar. 2008, www.flickr.com/photos/snorkmaiden/2334894536. Accessed 4 Jan. 2021.

Marlie. (2012, December 7). *Crochet Owl Ornaments*. Flickr. https://www.flickr.com/photos/marlie_makynen/8252061211

mocoxmoco. "Crochet Teddy Bear." *Flickr*, 6 Nov. 2011, www.flickr.com/photos/77570613@N06/6801823564. Accessed 7 Jan. 2021.

OrangeZoo. "Amigurumi Panda with Bamboo." *Flickr*, 10 Apr. 2012, www.flickr.com/photos/lilymama/7066060533. Accessed 7 Jan. 2021.

Pequeño Dino. *Flickr*, 15 Sept. 2017, www.flickr.com/photos/ournew/36853871273. Accessed 7 Jan. 2021.

Polino, Michelle. "*Crochet therapy.*" *ACA-ACC Professional Information Library*, [n.d.], https://www.counseling.org/docs/default-source/aca-acc-creative-activities-clearinghouse/crochet-therapy.pdf?sfvrsn=6. Accessed 1 Jan. 2021.

Rae. (2013, June 24). *Crochet octopus top*. Flickr. https://www.flickr.com/photos/sisterrae/9135000991

Ros, Vanesa. "Pollito." *Flickr*, 23 May 2012, www.flickr.com/photos/vanesaros/7254812172. Accessed 4 Jan. 2021.

Rou, Wen. "León." *Flickr*, 13 May 2012, www.flickr.com/photos/ournew/7192005212. Accessed 7 Jan. 2021.

Rou, Wen. "Reno." *Flickr*, 17 Dec. 2017, www.flickr.com/photos/ournew/39293965922. Accessed 7 Jan. 2021.

Saritha. "Caterpillar." *Flickr*, 13 May 2011, www.flickr.com/photos/58332759@N03/5946964878. Accessed 4 Jan. 2021.

Solmuteoriaa. "Two Mice." *Flickr*, 10 June 2017, www.flickr.com/photos/solmuteoriaa/41229557671. Accessed 4 Jan. 2021.

streinerte, sandija. "Tīģerīc…" *Flickr*, 1 Nov. 2009, www.flickr.com/photos/sandijastreinerte/4064005710. Accessed 7 Jan. 2021.

"Tiny Rhino." *Flickr*, 17 Jan. 2013, www.flickr.com/photos/sidrunszoo/8625624108. Accessed 4 Jan. 2021.

Tullus, Kristi. "Tiny Hippo." *Flickr*, 18 Jan. 2013, www.flickr.com/photos/sidrunszoo/8625624292. Accessed 4 Jan. 2021.

Yeung, L. (2017, September 21). *Happy Jellyfish Amigurumi Keychain Free Crochet Pattern*. Flickr. https://www.flickr.com/photos/coolcreativity/37208169812

Wales, Helen. "Crochet Bee." *Flickr*, 16 Apr. 2015, www.flickr.com/photos/heleninwales/22765827034. Accessed 7 Jan. 2021.

Printed in Poland
by Amazon Fulfillment
Poland Sp. z o.o., Wrocław